Child Training Tips

What I wish I knew when my children were young

EXPANDED EDITION

Reb Bradley

Family Ministries Publishing
Sheridan, California

Family Ministries Publishing
PO Box 266
Sheridan, California 95681
www.familyministries.com

Printed in the United States

All Bible quotes:
New International Version unless otherwise stated

To my wife, Beverly,
and the gifts God has given me:
Nathanael, Anna, Benjamin, Leah,
Michael, and Emily Claire

Acknowledgments

I thank the Lord for my wife, Beverly, who has been my partner in childrearing. As a fulltime mother she has not only spent more time training our children than I, but she gave many hours reviewing and suggesting edits on the rough draft manuscripts for this book.

I also thank the Lord for my children who endured my limited fatherhood during writing seasons.

I am thankful for Rick Fugate, whom I consider my mentor. It was his book and video series, "What the Bible Says About Child Training," which God used to give me the foundation for biblically-based child training I so desperately needed for my family. Without his teaching, I dread to think of where my children would be.

I am thankful for the parents of Hope Chapel who, year after year, sat through Rick Fugate's video series with me and gave their input in the many discussions that followed. And I am thankful for Mark Keathley, who was gracious enough to paint the cover for this edition.

I especially thank the Lord for giving us His Word, our only reliable source of Truth.

Contents

This book does **NOT** have all the answers on child training. It does however, contain answers to many of the questions I had when my oldest children were young. I have encountered many parents asking the same questions, so it became only natural to offer in written form the answers I have found over the years. At this writing, my three oldest are grown and married, but I still have three at home, so I am looking forward to adding to this work as they grow. I am presently writing a sequel, "Child Training Tips II," which I hope to make available before I have grandchildren.

Those looking for a manual, balanced in all facets of rearing children, will not find it here. The purpose of this book is simply to expose to parents possible blind spots, and to offer practical tips and biblically-based help in overcoming them. For a more balanced study on biblical parenting, I recommend[1] the audio or video presentation of my seminar, **Biblical Insights Into Child Training**. The seminar covers many of the same topics as this book, but includes stories and illustrations that help humanize the parenting process. It also includes tips for cultivating love relationships with your children.

---

[1] Also, for those who have not yet discovered it, the most foundational book available on biblical discipline of children is "What the Bible Says About Child Training." Published by Foundation for Biblical Research, J. Richard Fugate

I have written this book in outline form because I meant it to be a quick-reference manual. However, because of its outline style, some of my points are stated briefly, making it possible for them to be misunderstood. It is my hope that those parents who stumble over a few unclear points may not disregard the help offered in the balance of the book. Also, the reader will notice that some points are repeated in different sections. This is because each point is pertinent to its context.

After receiving overwhelming response to the first editions of this book, I am excited to publish this *expanded* edition. Multitudes of parents have written and told us of how their children changed when they began implementing the insights they gained. We are grateful to God for that. Yet, despite the positive response, I have decided to offer a caution to a certain "type" of parent before they begin reading.

So to those of you who might be *intense* parents – who already run your homes with a firm hand, I offer the following caution: Be forewarned! As you read the pages that follow, you will gain new insights into your children's motives and behavior, and you may find your usual anger and intolerance, growing in intensity the more you read. If that is you, then go slow! Watch your anger.

Keep in mind that our children are a product of our training, whether by intent or neglect. They are only the way they are, because we have not yet finished their training. If the children are not learning fast enough, and the training does not seem to be working, then it is time to look for blind spots in our approach, and not time for greater harshness. Keep in mind

God's word to us through James, *"... the anger of man does not accomplish the righteousness of God."*[2] Children respond best to alert, loving, consistent discipline – not to angry, "don't mess with me, kid" parenting.

I especially want to encourage everyone to hang in there to the end of this book and read chapter 15, the new chapter that qualifies this as an "expanded edition." I originally began writing the chapter "Beyond Obedience: Raising Children who Love God and Others," to be part of the sequel, but after hearing how some parents were becoming imbalanced in the area of love and discipline, I decided to include it in the original.

May all of us as parents seek God for the insight, self discipline and consistency we need to successfully raise the next generation to be mature, responsible followers of Christ. Amen.

Reb Bradley

---

[2] James 1:20

INTRODUCTION

"Children today are tyrants. They contradict their parents, they gobble their food, they terrorize their teachers."   Socrates - 426 BC

The job of parenting has always been a difficult one, but those who have lived in America for the last 40 years have watched it become even more so. Our children are faced with the influence of a declining morality, and as parents we are less confident than our predecessors in our knowledge of raising them. With the "experts" offering contradictory advice and the lack of a cohesive, biblical consensus within the Church, Christian parents have found themselves feeling helpless and frustrated with their children. For many of them, parenting has become such a source of frustration that they do everything within their power to prevent the conception of any more "problems." Their stress is so great that they count the days until their children are old enough to go to school or move out on their own. They look forward to summertime and holiday vacations, but dread the thought of being with their children all day long.

Those parents who are exasperated with their children are missing the blessing that God says children are to bring to their lives. They do not perceive children as a gift, but a *curse*. Fortunately, it does not have to be that way. When God calls children a "blessing," a "gift," and a "reward,"[3] He places each one in the womb with that potential. If our children are not a blessing to us, it is *not* because an alien tampered with their genetic code as they grew in the womb. It is, most likely, because we have not succeeded in some element of their training.

Considering the confusion of contemporary child rearing ideas and the sparse number of solid role models, it is no wonder that we have so many blind spots today. The tragedy is many frustrated parents believe they are doing everything correctly and think they have no blind spots. *But that is what a blind spot is – something you cannot see!*

One thing is certain, any parents who disclaim any responsibility for how their children may turn out, are depriving themselves of the potential they have to shape their children's character and future. May we all be open to see ourselves and our children in the pages that follow.

---

[3] Psalms 127:3-5

1

Six Obstacles to Successful Parenting

"I have seen the enemy and he are us."
Opus, Bloom County

Before we begin our study in parenting, it will be important for us to identify any obstacles that keep our blind spots hidden. I offer the following 6 obstacles, which if removed, will allow the reader to find greater value in this book.

Obstacle 1 – Parental Defensiveness

Regarding our personal lives, many of us recognize our weak human condition and are open to correction from others. However, should someone suggest something is wrong with our children or our parenting, that humility may disappear – we can become highly defensive!

In fact, merely the *suggestion* that we are defensive will cause some of us to immediately defend ourselves. *(Some, at this point, are inevitably defending themselves in their minds. If that is YOU, you may be completely unaware that you are resisting it right now! Blind aren't we!)*

In order to gain the most from this book, it will be helpful for you to drop your defenses, and admit that you have blind spots and cannot identify them. *(If you knew what they were, they wouldn't be "blind" spots, they would be "seen" spots!)* One of the main signs of a blind spot is defensiveness. If you read something in this book that contradicts your beliefs or practices, and you *immediately* defend yourself, or attack me, the author, you should consider that your toes have been stepped on and you do not like it. Possibly, you are *unwilling* to even consider that you need to change. You might not actually be wrong, but your intense resistance to "being wrong" could be a sign of defensiveness, which means you are closed to correction and therefore may miss receiving help with an area of weakness. As the Lord tells us through Solomon, it is the wise who welcome correction and reproof.[1] Let us be wise parents.

Before you continue, would you pause to look at the Lord, and ask Him to open the eyes of your heart?[2]

Obstacle 2 – Confusing *raising* children with *training* them

Many parents have the notion that *raising* children is the same as *training* them. It isn't. "Raising" is providing food and sustenance. It is maintaining life and fostering physical growth. The Scriptures call us not only to raise children, but also to *train* them. Those parents who believe they have carried out the biblical injunctions to train their children, yet the children remain unchanged, may have raised and *taught* their children, but they certainly did not succeed

---

[1] Prov 9:9; 12:1; 13:1, 18; 15:5, 12, 32; 19:25
[2] Eph 1:18

in *training* them. By the very definition of "train" that would be impossible.

To train means to *cause a change* in the one being directed. In any place of employment, if a training session is over, but the participants cannot do the job, they are not regarded as *trained*. They may have been taught, but they were not trained. The man who entrusts his dog to a dog-handler for training, but receives it back no different than it was before training, would be due a refund because the dog had not been successfully trained.

The Hebrew word for "rear" (gadal) bears out this concept. To *rear* a child literally means *"to twist unto greatness."* The Hebrew idea of rearing children was to bring them up to maturity by *twisting* them against their nature. Twisting requires firm effort, sustained throughout their childhood.

Proverbs 22:6 tells us that long-lasting change requires diligent training. Deuteronomy 6:6-9 reinforces this idea as it admonishes parents to impress God's commands on their children. The Hebrew word for *impress* means "to inscribe or etch." According to verses 7-9 this is accomplished by modeling and minute-by-minute instruction in biblical Truths, making on them a lasting *impression.*

Parents will never succeed who think that proper training of children consists only of playing Christian music tapes to them, and teaching them to pray before bedtime and meals. Nor will children be trained by simply sending them to Sunday School, youth groups, or Christian clubs. Surrounding them with Christian influences is certainly good, but it is no substitute for "training." Training is a conscious, active effort of instruction, discipline, and modeling, and not a byproduct of a good environment or a loving home. It does not happen by osmosis. Consider that no wild horse was ever broken or trained by being grouped together with trained horses. Neither will be our children. (Please do not be offended at the comparison of training horses and children – the Hebrew words and the principles are the same.)

Obstacle 3 – **Misunderstanding human depravity**

One dangerous, humanistic idea which has crept into the Church, is that children are basically good and need only be loved and cared for to bring out that good. This view not only ignores the basic teaching of Scripture, but also encourages parents to let a child's nature take its own course. That is tantamount to taking a wild skunk as a pet, believing it will never release its stench because of the good home you will give it. The Bible teaches that allowing a self-centered heart to take its natural course guarantees trouble.[3]

God has spoken clearly in the Scriptures about the depraved nature of humanity. Jeremiah 17:9 tells us that *"the heart is deceitful above all things and beyond cure."* King David, a man after God's own heart, said in Psalm 51:5 that he was *"sinful at birth, sinful from the time my mother conceived me,"* and he declared that from birth we go astray, even coming out of the womb "speaking lies."[4]

---

[3] Prov 29:15 The rod of correction imparts wisdom, but a child left to himself disgraces his mother.
[4] Ps 58:3

For parents to successfully train children they must understand Proverbs 22:15: *"Foolishness is bound up in the heart of a child..."* The Hebrew word for foolishness is *'ivveleth*, which does not mean childish immaturity or silliness, but rather *perversity,* which spawns *deviousness, defiance,* and *rebellion.* In describing adults who grew up without proper training, Solomon called them "fools"[5] using the word *keciyl,* which, in its root, means "fat." By nature we are all born *fat with ourselves.* The parents who think their child is just a little angel and would rarely do anything really wrong, will not adequately apply themselves to the task of child training and are guaranteed by the Scriptures to reap grief in the years to come. Consider Solomon's words: *"A foolish son brings grief to his father and bitterness to the one who bore him."*[6] *"To have a fool for a son brings grief; there is no joy for the father of a fool."*[7] *"... a child left to himself disgraces his mother."*[8] For further study on human nature, consider also: Gen 6:5; 8:21; Eccl 7:20,29; Ps 14:2-3; Job 4:17-19; 15:15-16; 25:4-6; Is 59:7; 64:6; Jer 13:23; Mark 7:20-23; John 2:24-25; Rom 3:10-18; 7:18.

Although God's Word is a sufficient source for understanding a child's depraved nature, it is interesting to note the conclusions of the Minnesota Crime Commission which issued the following report after

---

[5] Prov 10:1; 15:20; 17:21, 25; 19:13
[6] Prov 17:25
[7] Prov 17:21
[8] Prov 29:15

years of studying the relationship of environment to crime:

> *"Every baby starts life as a little savage. He is completely selfish and self-centered. He wants what he wants when he wants it: his bottle, his mother's attention, his playmate's toys, his uncle's watch, or whatever. Deny him these and he seethes with rage and aggressiveness which would be murderous were he not so helpless. He's dirty, he has no morals, no knowledge, no developed skills. This means that all children, not just certain children, but all children are born delinquent. If permitted to continue in their self-centered world of infancy, given free reign to their impulsive actions to satisfy every want, every child would grow up a criminal, a thief, a killer, a rapist."*

The parents who desire to see their children grow in godly character must not assume it will happen because they are being raised in a loving Christian home. Successful training of a self-centered child requires hard work, great personal sacrifice, and prayer.

Obstacle 4 – Ignorance of parental responsibilities

Most parents discover soon after the birth of their first child that parenting is a tremendous responsibility. They feel the weight of caring for a helpless human being, but are often ignorant of their actual job description. As the child grows, they hope they are doing their job correctly, but may find the child is not turning out the way they thought he would. Most parents are like employees who are hired to do a job, but have minimal training, no job descriptions, no plans, and no measurable objectives.

To become an effective child trainer requires that a parent understand exactly what God expects them to produce in their children and how they are to achieve those results. This book should be an aid to formulating a parental job description.

Obstacle 5 – Trust in worldly "experts"

As children of God we have been given the Scriptures as our only reliable source of absolute truth.[9] The world offers many ideas it regards to be "true," but the Bible is the one standard for determining what is *actually* True. The Word encapsulates our knowledge of God, and is the means by which He has given us *"everything we need for life and godliness."*[10] For basic parenting principles therefore, we must look primarily to God's Word. To look elsewhere guarantees trouble.

Psalms 1:1 tells us that we will be blessed if we do not seek advice from those without Christ. Although they have the appearance of wisdom and offer insights that may seem reasonable, their thinking is infected with worldliness, and leads to regret.[11] The apostle Paul emphasized this when he pointed out that those without Christ lack genuine wisdom, and what they offer as valuable, God regards as worthless.[12] He says that *"... the wisdom of this world is foolishness in God's sight ... the thoughts of the wise are vain."*[13] That should not surprise us, considering that God tells us that those lacking the fear of God, whether professing Christian or not, are hampered in their

---

[9] 2 Tim 3:16
[10] 2 Pet 1:3
[11] Prov 16:25
[12] 1 Cor 1:19-25
[13] 1 Cor 3:19-20

thinking and do not have even the basics of wisdom.[14] These warnings are validated by America's present condition. The breakdown of the family and the resulting corruption of our society is partially a result of the last few generations receiving guidance from worldly "experts." Like the rest of American society, families within the Church are also in decline, because Christian leaders have undiscerningly received "wisdom" from the world's experts, then Christianized it, and passed it on to the Church.

With God's Word offering such an abundant resource of absolute Truth and godly wisdom, we must draw our basic principles for child training strictly from the Bible. Although most Christians will quickly agree with this premise, many are unaware of the worldly ideas they have incorporated into their parenting. It would therefore benefit parents to reevaluate and determine the validity of their present child training philosophies in light of biblical principles.

As an example, worldly experts observe rebellion in 2 year olds and deduce that all children naturally go through a phase that they label the "terrible twos." They then encourage parents to not be concerned, but to patiently wait for the phase to run its course. When that child is still defiant at age 3, the concerned parents are told not to worry, because the child is simply going through a phase called the "trying threes." When the child is still willful and demanding at adolescence, the parents are told that it is a transitory prepubescent phase, but will eventually pass. By the time the child becomes a teenager, his parents already believe the

---

[14] Prov 9:10; 1:7; Psa 111:10

modern idea that teens are naturally rebellious and independent from their families. They endure disrespectful attitudes hoping that their teen will grow out of his self-absorption before their hearts break.

Sadly, many parents accept from the "experts" that these phases are natural and unavoidable. They expect them and endure them, not realizing that God's Word not only does not recognize any such "phases" of rebellion which should be tolerated, but teaches parents how to prevent rebellion. Those who choose not to accept modern phases in their children and instead, implement biblical principles, discover that their children never go through them. One must conclude that the experts who developed ideas about childhood "phases" studied only poorly trained children. At the least, they did not take into consideration that these phases are common to this century and primarily to affluent nations like America.

Upon hearing biblical principles taught, some parents wrestle with accepting them. If that is you, then as you read, listen to your reason for your struggle. Is it that you believe the Bible teaches something different? Is it that you dispute the meaning of the Hebrew words cited? Or could it be that you have based your convictions on human ideas and worldly principles? As God's people we must grow in our knowledge and application of God's Word, and base our convictions on its precepts. Parenting practices, rooted in any other premise, will always fail. As you read that which follows, may you take to heart that which comes from God's Word – the rest, consider seriously.

Obstacle 6 – Fear of repeating one's own past negative childhood

Some parents approach child training with a "vendetta." They are out to right the wrongs they experienced as children themselves. The frustration they feel from their childhood memories, however, often creates a blind spot. Consequently, biblical elements of child training may be inadvertently avoided, because they seem too much like what they endured.

A parent's vendetta may be rooted in a variety of childhood hurts:

- The adult who grew up in a poor family is determined to indulge his children with all that he did not have, yet cannot now understand why they are turning out self-centered and ungrateful.

- The adult who was never allowed to play or do social activities as a child, may require little work of his own children, and may overindulge them with sports and recreation. He then wonders why they are lazy or preoccupied with themselves and their personal gratification.

- The adult whose parents were too strict or abusive is tempted to be too permissive with his own children, despite the clear teaching of Scripture.

- The adult who was never allowed to speak his mind to his parents, takes the opposite approach in his home, and then finds he is raising sassy, smart-mouthed children.

- The adult who was never given wisdom behind parental commands, is determined with his own children to offer full explanations before they are expected to obey. Yet, finds that as his children grow, they are unable to obey without arguing, his explanations seeming to serve as invitations to debate.

The poor training of any child is a tragic thing, but it is made worse when that child grows up and hurts his own children by trying too hard to do the opposite of what was done to him. Those parents who were victims of poor training are right to avoid the mistakes made by their parents, but they must guard themselves from rejecting solid biblical principles, just because they seem *close* to what they experienced. If our parents' approach *seemed* close to biblical parenting, yet bore bad fruit, we can be certain it was not biblical. God preserved in His Word exactly the right principles we need for training children, and parents who accurately implement them will not be disappointed. In fact, they will be blessed.

2

Goals of Child Training

Fathers, do not exasperate your children; instead, **bring them up** *in the training and instruction of the Lord.* Ephesians 6:4

One of the biggest problems for parents today is that they work hard at training and instructing their children about the Lord and His ways, but lack a clearly defined goal for that training. They know they want their children to know God and to have godly character, but they are not sure what the final product is supposed to look like. It is as though they are baking a dessert, yet don't know if it is an ice cream cake or a peach cobbler, and they keep throwing in sweet ingredients, hoping the results will be edible. It would be far better for parents to define their goal and then create a plan to accomplish it. There is truth to the saying, "If you aim at nothing, you will always hit it." Christian parents must have a clearly defined target for their children's growth.

In order to determine if we are accomplishing God's goals for child rearing we must first identify them. As Christian parents our most obvious goal is to bring our children to salvation. Second to that, God's most basic goal for training children is encapsulated in Ephesians 6:4. There, parents are told regarding their children, *"...bring them up in the training and instruction of* the Lord." The Greek word for "bring them up" holds the key. That word is ektrepho, which means: *to rear up to maturity.* The primary goal then, of training and instruction, is to rear up children to *maturity.* For us to bring children to maturity will require that we have a clear definition of what maturity is.

WHAT IS MATURITY?

Based on a broad study of the Old Testament and a concentrated study of Proverbs, it is clear that maturity is characterized by 3 elements: ***self-control,***[1] ***wisdom,***[2] and ***responsibility,***[3] which can be defined as follows:

- **Self-control:** not being ruled by passions, emotions, desires, wishes, or curiosity; freedom from having to do what one feels like doing; the ability to choose to do what is right; fosters the *selflessness* necessary for love of others.

- **Wisdom:** understanding; insight; ability to learn from experience; ability to make sound decisions; handling stressful problems with a level head; possible only when not ruled by passions (self-controlled)

- **Responsibility:** accepting personal accountability for one's own actions, as well as faithful and conscientious work habits; such integrity and reliability are possible only when not ruled by passions (self-controlled)

---

[1] Prov 29:11; 14:16; 21:20; 22:15; 26:11; 12:16, 23; 13:16; 29:20
[2] Prov 10:21; 29:15; 17:16; 18:2; 12:15
[3] Prov 17:16; 6:6; 24:30; 26:6; 26:16

HOW IS MATURITY DEVELOPED?

Maturity is rooted primarily in self-control which, in turn, facilitates growth in wisdom and responsibility. The most basic objective of training children, therefore, is the subduing of their self-will. From the time children are born, parents must develop in them the ability to say "NO" to their own desires and "YES" to their parents. That is why parental control of young children is imperative. A child who learns to deny his own desires and submit to his parent's controls, gains inner controls. Children are born into the world self-centered, and so must be trained from infancy that the world does not revolve around them. They must learn that life will not always give them their way. Susanna Wesley, who raised 9 children, including John and Charles Wesley, put it this way:

> *"The parent who studies to subdue [self-will] in his child works together with God in the renewing and saving a soul. The parent who indulges it does the devil's work, makes religion impossible, salvation unattainable, and does all that in him lies to damn his child, soul and body forever."*[4]

The child whose will is never subdued when young, comes to believe that he should have *what* he wants, *when* he wants it, and should not have to endure *anything* he does not like. He will grow older thinking he is being deprived whenever he does not get what he wants from life, and by his teen years he will become preoccupied with his "rights" and know little of personal responsibility. The indulged child is frequently

---

[4] The Journal of John Wesley [Chicago: Moody, n. d.] p.106

angry because he does not get what he thinks is owed him. Ultimately, he will develop a "victim" mentality – nothing is ever his fault – someone else is always to blame for his misery.

Some parents believe that maturity is an inevitable part of growing up and will happen naturally to all children, whether trained or not. Proper rearing of children, in their view, requires only that a parent love them, take them to church, and try to give them a happy childhood. To them, maturity is a guaranteed byproduct of getting older, so they do little to help the process, and without realizing it – much to hurt it. All children, unless calamity occurs, *will* grow older, but only those groomed toward maturity will attain it. Hence, as parents, we must work diligently to help our children develop the qualities leading to maturity.

WHAT CHARACTERIZES IMMATURITY?

To further clarify the definition of maturity, we must understand *immaturity*. The child whose will is not subdued in the first few years of life is hampered in the maturing process. No matter how old he gets, a strong self-will ruled by the craving for *self-indulgence* will be the mark of his immaturity. Sadly, this self-indulgence characterizes most children today – even in Christian families. As caring parents it is especially important for us to identify and eliminate that in our child rearing which feeds the will and fosters self-indulgence in our children.

WHAT ARE THE SIGNS OF IMMATURITY AND SELF-INDULGENCE?

Self-indulgence is the drive which demands the satisfaction of one's wants and desires. Consider the following symptom list. Do these symptoms generally characterize your children?

They are indulged if they lack self-control

- Self-indulgent people rarely say "NO" to themselves.

- They have a difficult time doing in moderation anything which gratifies; they frequently over-do-it.

- They do whatever they feel like, or are so used to having their way that they think they *should* have whatever they want.

- The satisfaction of their *own* will is foremost in their life – others are considered second, if at all.

They are indulged if they are self-absorbed

- Self-centeredness so rules self-indulgent people that they live as if the world revolved around them – life is interpreted by how it affects *them*.

- Whenever the self-centered child approaches his parents with a question, (which may be frequent), it usually involves something he wants for himself. He has few sincere questions regarding the well being of others.

- One who is self-consumed, pushes and lobbies parents constantly to get what is wanted; persists even after being refused.

- May think of others, but only after satisfying themselves.

- Insists on his "rights" to personal decisions and "living his own life."
- Think they deserve everything that is given to them, and are unappreciative despite the feelings of others; not easily satisfied.
- They are seldom happy; complain and whine a majority of the time; often discontent.
- Complain about food or any gift set before them.
- They are preoccupied with fun and self-gratification.
- Expect for life to be exciting; demand entertainment; frequently bored.
- Expect to have their own way; express blatant irritation when desires are thwarted.
- Impatient; demand others' immediate attention.

They are indulged if they lack wisdom

- Their desire for gratification rules them, affecting all of their decisions and actions; they are impulsive and lack discretion.
- They consistently squander money (or save it with the intent of spending it on themselves.)
- They do not learn from their mistakes; they repeatedly get into trouble for the same offense.
- They cannot be left alone and trusted to make wise choices.
- In response to attacks and offenses from younger siblings, they retaliate as if they were small children themselves.

- When confronted by problems, they foolishly "bury their heads in the sand" and pretend the problem will go away.

They are indulged if they are irresponsible

- When they sin, they habitually deny their responsibility.

- Nothing is ever their fault. They always see themselves as a victim of others' failures. Someone or something else is to blame.

- When they get caught for breaking the rules, they do not see their penalty as a consequence of their choices, but hold responsible the one who caught them or turned them in.

- Even their anger is someone else's fault.

- They resent work or anything that requires self-discipline.

- They are lazy; they habitually play during chore time, and look for ways to get out of work.

- They despise opportunities to serve others, particularly their siblings.

- The thought of serving others rarely crosses their mind.

- In response to assigned chores – roll their eyes; complain; disappear – before, during and after task; do as little as possible.

- After completion of assigned tasks, refuse to ask, "Is there anything more I can do?"

Some parents read a list like this and respond with excitement – their children are on the right path!

Others, however, respond with discouragement – they *thought* their children were heading in a good direction, but now realize they are off course. PARENTS – do not despair! Thank the Lord for a timely course correction. Yes, there is work to be done, but effort invested into developing maturity is never wasted.

USING THE GOAL OF MATURITY AS A BASIS FOR PARENTAL DECISIONS

To restate our premise – a proper understanding of maturity and immaturity is foundational to effective parenting, for without a clear understanding of the goals of parenting we have no frame of reference for parental decisions. To evaluate our parenting decisions we need simply determine: *What will this activity, organization, or relationship, foster within our children – maturity or immaturity?* It is really that simple.

The problem is that as modern American parents we have come to believe the misnomer that children will eventually reach maturity by themselves, and little input from us is needed. Rather than making *maturity* our primary goal for them, we mistakenly substitute as a goal – *a happy and fulfilling childhood.* Consequently, from the time our children are born, we feed their desire for self-indulgence and accidentally keep them immature. By the time they reach their teen years they are just like the other "normal" self-involved teenagers whose parents also made a fun childhood *their* chief goal. Since so many American parents indulge their children, America is filled with immature, gratification-oriented teenagers. National researchers and experts, not realizing that teenage rebellion and self-absorption is a phenomena of this century, and unique to only a few affluent nations like ours, have concluded such behavior is a natural and temporary phase of growing up. Parents expect it and accept it. Most teens do grow up, but sadly, too few become mature.

Although most of us as parents love our children, our commitment to their happiness harms them. Indulged children are unprepared for adulthood. They have been sent the message that their personal happiness is of supreme importance, so they grow up thinking it is owed them. They ultimately lack the self-discipline necessary for successful employment, and their self-centeredness will cause strife in their marriages. Then when their marriages fail, they will not consider it their fault – they will be innocent "victims" of their spouse's shortcomings. From the time they are young, our children must learn that life is not about fun and entertainment, nor is it about personal happiness and self-gratification. It is about responsibility and serving others. It is finding joy in honoring God and loving our neighbors.[5]

WHAT HAS LIFE TAUGHT US?

Those of us who have lived at least 25 years have learned that *life is hard – things don't always go our way – we don't always get what we want in life*. Our children must be prepared in their youth for the challenges they will find in life. They must learn that they cannot have everything they want, and that they can endure quite well with less than they hoped for. To

---

[5] In chapter 15 these ideas will be further developed.

mature properly, children must learn while they are still toddlers to obey their parents quickly and without resistance, and to endure hard situations humbly. With their parents' help, they can learn as early as possible to die to themselves,[6] preparing them to live for Christ. Otherwise, as teenagers, they will remain self-consumed, rebellious, and far from God. May we as parents be faithful to do what is right.

---

[6] Col 3:5; Rom 12:1; 8:13; 6:6-8, 13; 1 Cor 9:26-27; Gal 5:24; Titus 2:12; Eph 4:22; Mat 16:24-26; Luke 14:26

3

Establishing Control
in the Home

When the Duke of Windsor was asked what impressed him most in America, he replied, *"The way American parents obey their children."*

Today, some parents are afraid to keep their children under control, because "controlling" others is purported to be a psychological "no no" – *controlling*, they have heard, is "abusing." No, it is not abusive to control children – it is biblical, and therefore wise.

The fifth commandment requires children to honor and obey their parents.[1] The responsibility to enforce this command falls to the parents, so it is their job to exercise firm control over their children and train them to be obedient.

God considers parental control of children to be so important, and such a basic evidence of spiritual maturity, that a man is deemed unqualified to serve in a ministry capacity unless his children are obedient and well controlled.[2] In the Old Testament, both Samuel and Eli lost their ministries because their sons were not under their control. King David's throne was almost taken by his son Adonijah, because David did not assert

---

[1] Ex 20:12; Deu 5:16; Eph 6:1-3
[2] 1 Tim 3:4-5; Titus 1:6

proper control over him growing up.[1] In ancient Israel, in fact, God regarded parental control as so important that He decreed by civil law, that teenage children who were out of control were to be publicly executed.[2] Yes, parental control is not only possible, but also *imperative*.

WHAT IS A CONTROLLED CHILD?

A controlled child is one who has submitted his will to his parents. When they speak to him he obeys them quickly and with a good attitude – even when they are not watching. He has self-control, and so obeys them without sass or complaint.

ESTABLISHING PARENTAL CONTROL

Why does God deem it important to train children to submit without question to parental authority?

1. The optimum success of any training requires that the will of the trainee be submitted to the trainer.

2. A child trained to submit to *outer* controls gains *inner* controls.

3. Children who lack firm boundaries, and are allowed to push and whine, constantly voicing their opinions about discipline, personal duties, or family decisions, are actually being permitted to assume responsibility for running the home – a task for which God has not equipped their small shoulders.

---

[1] 1 Sam 3:13-14; 8:3; 1 Kings1:5-6
[2] Ex 21:17; Lev 20:9; De 21:18-21; 27:16; Prov 1:8; 20:20; 30:17; Mat 15:4

4. The stress from running the home and testing the limits causes children to have a generally unhappy disposition. Consistently required obedience creates firm boundaries, thereby removing stress and giving children a sense of security and peace.

5. A child used to pushing and getting his own way at home has greater difficulty in submitting to any authority outside the home.

6. Quick obedience to parental authority must be learned to insure safety in times of danger.

7. The child who has learned submission to human authority more easily submits to God's authority.

Adults who profess faith in Christ, yet do not obey Him without question and yield to His authority, very likely grew up without learning to submit quickly to authority. They were trained to resist authority themselves, by not being required to obey it. Their well-meaning parents may have actually succeeded in *strengthening* their will, by challenging it, but never actually conquering it. Every time parents attempt to exercise authority, but give in to the resistance of their child, they subtly reward him for bucking authority and strengthen his will in the process. Those parents, by not exercising their authority, ultimately make theirs a child-run home.

WHAT IS A "CHILD-RUN" HOME?

A child-run home is one in which all decisions are made or influenced by the children. Typically, in such a home, parents feel obligated to allow their children a voice in most family matters.

IDENTIFYING A "CHILD-RUN" HOME

Parents in a child-run home will be heard saying things like:

- "I can't make that for dinner at our house, the kids just won't eat it."

- "I prepare meals in two batches – one for my husband and I, and one cooked a special way for the kids."

- "Among restaurants, my wife and I enjoy Sizzlers, but we never go there ... the kids prefer the playland at McDonalds."

- "We can't have that family over to the house, their children are so much younger than ours. Ours would not enjoy them."

- "We can't go there, the kids will be bored!"

- "We can never go out. Our children just don't behave for baby-sitters."

- "We could never take our children into the church service. They wouldn't last."

- "We won't be able to attend. Our little Princess just doesn't do well in those situations."

- "We'll have to find a new church. Junior just doesn't get along with one of the boys in his class."

- "We'll have to change teachers or schools. Little Jane doesn't enjoy Mrs. So & So."

Those parents who say, "Junior just refuses to ...," or "My child just won't put up with ..." have given up their authority and put their children in charge of their home. They have granted their children veto power and in doing so must follow their children's leadership. Needless to say, for those parents who have shared their authority with their children, parenting will be very difficult and unfruitful.

Parents share their authority with their children for several reasons:

- They may be exercising what some call "democratic parenting." The basis for this approach is that since children are people, with opinions and preferences, they should have rights to influence all decisions affecting them. The error of this kind of thinking is obvious. To grow in maturity, and to be prepared for "real life" (which does not give them a say in everything), children need to learn self-control by submitting themselves to their parents' control. They must learn that what they want does not absolutely have to happen, and that they can survive quite well without expressing their opinion or getting their way.

- Some parents are "child-centered" in their parenting. They want their children to have a happy and fulfilling childhood, so make all decisions based on their children's desires. Since they live for their children's happiness, their goal is to minimize the challenges their children might face, and make life as fun and entertaining as possible. Parents of this type strive to please their children, but find them never satisfied and rarely appreciative.

- The primary reason that parents give away their authority is that they are insecure and crave their children's approval. They try to make their children happy and seek to avoid disappointing them, because they want to be liked. However, their need for their children's love often has the opposite effect – they become despicable to their children. Ultimately, insecure parents become intimidated by their own children, and therefore are hampered in giving strong leadership.

IDENTIFYING AN INTIMIDATED PARENT

Intimidated parents . . .

- Need their children's approval.
- Dread making their children mad at them.
- Say, in their hearts, *"Please don't hate me."*
- Conclude most parental commands with, "Okay?"
- Strive to talk their children into obedience by laying out extensive arguments with each command.
- Become exasperated from nagging and trying to persuade children to comply with directions.
- Instead of chastising for rebellious anger, try to diffuse it with distractions or the offering of treats.
- Find themselves trying to gain their children's approval and permission before administering chastisement, by extensive explaining and apologizing for disciplinary actions; to keep their child's affection, they strive to be understood.
- Hastily lavish affection on the child, rubbing their little bottom immediately after a spanking, because they fear their child's rejection.
- Fear rejection after administering chastisement, so offer treats to regain lost affection.

41

- Allow children to freely express their opinions, complaints, and criticisms regarding family decisions.

THE IMPORTANCE OF HAVING YOUR CHILDREN'S RESPECT

We as adults do not learn well from those we do not respect, whether it is our pastor, our boss, or our spouse. Children, for the same reason, will not submit themselves to our training if we lose their respect. The parents whose home is child-run have already lost their children's respect and must regain it.[3]

TIPS ON REGAINING AUTHORITY AND EARNING YOUR CHILDREN'S RESPECT

- To gain respect, parents must cause their children to obey their word.

  A parent in charge of the home speaks a command one time, calmly and clearly, and is obeyed. If you continually threaten, but do not follow through with discipline, you will not regain your children's respect, and will only be contemptible to them. Consistent consequences must follow all disobedience.

- To regain lost respect, authority must be taken completely back, once and for all.

  The parent who shares authority with a child, and then occasionally attempts to take it back and exercise it, will only be resented.

---

[3] *How do you respect someone with authority who is afraid to exercise it?*

- Do not allow your child to argue with you, or show you any other disrespect.

  If they are in that habit, you have lost your authority already. You have permitted them to speak to you with the same disrespect they would show a peer, so when you exercise authority they will despise you.

- Watch out for the "Camp Counselor Syndrome."

  Parents who try to be their child's buddy or pal are like the stereotypical camp counselor who gets close to kids, but is not taken too seriously when exercising firm authority. Parents who try to be their child's pal, will often find the child resenting it when authority is exercised, illustrating the saying, "familiarity breeds contempt." Single parents, because they have no mate for friendship, are particularly susceptible to this temptation.[4]

- Do not use your size and authority to tease your children.

  You misuse it and in doing so, lose their trust and respect when you later try to exercise your authority.

- Aim primarily for their *respect* – not their *affection*.

  Those parents who *need* their children's love are crippled in their parenting by their own insecurities. Because insecure parents seek their child's love and approval to feel good about themselves, they cannot offer strong leadership. Their efforts to *give* their

---

[4] Trying to be their "buddy" is not to be confused with winning their hearts by gaining their trust. Children must be motivated by their love for us as well as their respect for our authority. More discussion on this in chapter 15.

children firm discipline and training are hampered by their efforts to gain *from* them acceptance. Children unconsciously sense their parents' need for their approval, and enjoy the power it gives them.

Parents, we must remember – **we** are the ones in charge of the home. We owe no apologies for the exercise of our authority. We are not answerable or accountable to our children, and must never seek their approval for our parenting. As long as we send the message that we need approval we will not succeed in controlling their behavior, they will not gain self-control, and we will not succeed in training them for Christ.

KEYS TO ESTABLISHING CONTROL

1. Keep your objective in mind – subjection of their will. Never forget that your overall objective of training is to develop in your children maturity, which means your goal is to give them the ability to say "No" to themselves.

2. Require quick obedience. Give instructions one time, calmly and clearly, and require immediate obedience with a good attitude. Bring a consequence if they do not obey.

3. Teach your children to obey without being told "why." It is imperative to shape a child's moral reasoning skills by telling him the wisdom behind parental commands, but it is important that children *first* learn to obey whether they understand "why" or not. Children who learn to obey without knowing "why" develop inner controls and submissive hearts that make them open to moral instruction from their parents.

WHY CHILDREN MUST LEARN TO OBEY WITHOUT KNOWING THE REASONS BEHIND THEIR PARENTS' INSTRUCTIONS

In the last 40 years parents have lost the vision of requiring children to obey them simply because they are the parents. These parents have developed the habit of trying to persuade children into obedience by offering lengthy explanations for every instruction they give. This has resulted in a generation who know little of quick obedience to authority and who habitually challenge every command not only at home, but also at school and in the workplace. Children must learn to obey their parents whether they understand "why" or not. Consider the following reasons:

- A chief characteristic of those in authority is that they are not accountable to those under their control. In fact, the first sign that they have lost control is that they feel the need to constantly explain themselves to those they oversee. Our children, therefore, must learn as toddlers that we will not attempt to talk them into obedience, by proving the value of every instruction.

- If you habitually justify your instructions, you will find yourself enduring your child's wrath if you fail to persuade him with your reasoning. Eventually, it will become his "right" to know your reasoning and agree with you before he will obey.

- If your goal is to *persuade* your child to obey, then he is not submitting to your authority – he is only doing what is reasonable to him. No self-control is exercised or learned.

WHY PARENTS SHOULD GIVE CHILDREN REASONS FOR OBEDIENCE

When a child has demonstrated that he can consistently obey without needing to be persuaded to do so, then he is ready to begin learning the wisdom behind parental commands. This means that parents will *occasionally* begin offering him a brief reason for obedience. As he grows and demonstrates he can still obey at the times no reasons are given, he shows himself ready to hear parental wisdom more often.

A parent's goal is to train children to become fully self-governing, motivated toward good behavior not by Mommy's prohibitions, but by well-developed personal values. This will require that parents give wisdom for parental commands much of the time, but not necessarily all of the time. The parent who occasionally offers no reason for obedience to their older children reinforces the importance of submitting to authority, whether reasons are understood or not.

AN EXAMPLE OF APPROPRIATE DIALOGUE WITH CHILDREN LEARNING THE WISDOM BEHIND PARENTAL INSTRUCTIONS:

Appropriate parental instructions

"Honey, please play on the other side of the house. The baby is sleeping and you might wake him."

Appropriate response

"Yes, Mom."

Inappropriate responses

"But I'll be quiet."

"But I usually play out here and he doesn't awaken."
"But I don't like it in the other side of the house."
"But it's time for him to wake up."
"You never let me have any fun."

Further help on teaching children to respond with respect can be found in chapter 9, "Raising Respectful Children."

GIVING REASONS WITHOUT INVITING ARGUMENTS

Children must be taught to make good decisions in life, but giving brief reasons for obedience does not mean offering *thorough explanations* at the time of the command. Many parents accidentally invite debate from their children by allowing a discussion of their reasoning at the moment obedience is required. Children should not be allowed to question your reasoning at that moment. This policy must be established early in their childhood, because it is difficult to retrain children who have been conditioned to expect a discussion and persuasive reasons for obeying. Children should be allowed to request clarification of parental directions, but not be allowed to engage them in debate.

When parents offer a brief statement of wisdom while giving instructions, children should be referred back to an earlier time of formal family instruction on godliness, or they should know a detailed explanation will come later. For example, the child who is told, *"Johnny, please play more quietly. Others are being disturbed by your noise,"* is merely being reminded of the biblical admonition to *"love your neighbor as yourself,"* and is expected to comply with the insights of his parents. If the situation is new, and Johnny does not understand the logic behind his parents' request, he should be able to respectfully obey and anticipate an explanation later during a parent-initiated time of family instruction.

WHAT ABOUT AN OLDER CHILD WHOSE WILL HAS NEVER BEEN SUBDUED AND HAS NOT BEEN TRAINED TO OBEY HUMBLY?

Many parents reading this book have older children whose wills were not brought into submission when they were young – they are full of themselves and voice their opinions about every command given them. Although they did not learn self-denial during their most formative years, it is not too late for them. Since their root need is to learn to say "No" to themselves, they must go back and learn to obey without discussion. Here's one possible plan:

- After finishing this book, you should approach them and apologize for failing to properly develop within them maturity and prepare them for adulthood.

- Explain how they must learn to humbly accept parental directions without always knowing the reasons why.

- Give them a time period for demonstrating quiet, humble obedience (perhaps 6-8 weeks[5]), during which all parental commands will be given without reasons, and no appeals will be considered.

---

[5] If an 18 year old rebel can learn to answer "Yes, Sir," and make a perfect bunk after a 6-week military boot camp, a 10 year old can learn to be respectful in the same amount of time.

- Tell them they will be required to respond, "Yes, Mom," or "Yes, Dad," to every command, unless it is an emergency. Only then, may they make an appeal.

- An emergency is defined as a time when they have no ability to carry out the command, or they know the parent giving the command lacks information which will most certainly affect the command given, ie: *The other parent has given a contradictory command; they have no transportation to go somewhere; there is insufficient food for preparation of a meal; the detergent box is empty, so clothes cannot be washed, etc.*

- Explain to them that if at the end of the time period, they consistently obey quickly and respectfully, then you will begin to give wisdom behind your commands.

- You must make clear to them, however, that when you begin sharing wisdom behind commands, it will not be the same as your former habits, when you allowed debates. The reasons you give will be brief and may not be discussed at the moment of instruction.

- If, at the end of the preset time period, they have not proven they can obey without question, then extend the period, and train them until they have gained self-control.

Keep in mind that as they grow and demonstrate they can submit unquestioningly to authority, you can entrust them with more reasons for obedience.

RESPECTFUL WAYS OF CHANGING A PARENT'S MIND

Although parents must be careful to not invite

discussion about every parental command, children who are humble and respectful in their attitude should have the opportunity to appeal parental decisions at times. The key to making an acceptable appeal is the respectful attitude in which it is made. Children must never be allowed to dishonor parents by responding with a raised voice, sass, or angry objection. Parents must be careful not to reward such disrespect by continuing the discussion. If children do not learn early in life to be self-controlled in their communication, they will become belligerent as teenagers and will lack self-restraint in all other relationships. Children should have the opportunity for appeals, but only if they demonstrate honor for their parents. More discussion on respectful appeals in chapter 9.

RESPONDING TO CHILDREN WHO ASK "WHY?"

A fundamental principle of child training is that children should not be permitted to respond continuously to parental commands with "Why?" Two primary reasons:

- It shows resistance to parental authority and delays immediate obedience.
- It is disrespectful. The appropriate responses to any parental directive are "Yes, Dad," "Sure, Mom," "May I appeal?," or possibly, "May I have your permission to ask why?" but never just, "Why?'

Keep in mind that there is nothing wrong with a child's desire to know his parents' reasoning. Curiosity is natural and children do need their moral values shaped by learning the wisdom behind parental commands. That which is disrespectful, however, is the quick *demand* to know "Why?." Such a challenge assumes a parent is accountable to a child. The child who *insists* they be told "why," must not be rewarded by hearing the reason.

Remember the biblical account of Job? Throughout his painful trial, he accused God of injustice, challenging His right to permit his suffering. Although God could have explained to Job His reasons for allowing the trial, He never did tell Job "why." He would not honor Job's disrespectful insistence on an answer.[6] Even after Job finally humbled himself and repented of his pride,[7] he received no answer from God. As parents we must follow God's example and not reward our children's disrespect.

Children who habitually ask "Why," when given a command, most likely do so, because their parents have offered them a reason for obedience and then allowed dialogue about it. By engaging in debate, parents become exasperated and either attempt to persuade with the logic of the command or come back with the ever brilliant response, *"Because I said so."* Of course *you* said so – they just heard you say it. What you really meant was that they should obey, because of your *parental authority*. The problem is that you should establish your authority early on in their life and never have to refer back to it. The very fact that you frequently remind them of your authority reinforces to them that you are not sure of it. Consider

---

[6] Even a righteous person like Job can become disrespectful of authority when he takes his eyes off the Lord and puts them on himself and his problems.

[7] Job 42:1-6

your dialogues in light of Proverbs 26:4-5[8]. (More discussion in chapter 5, "Nurturing Children With Discipline.")

Curiosity or avoidance?

Parents should consider that children usually do not ask "Why" because they desire to grow in wisdom, but because they want to debate their parents' reasoning, and thereby avoid obedience. Those children who respectfully ask the reason for a parental command should have the opportunity to discover their parents' wise reasoning, but *thorough* discussion should usually be permitted only *after* they have obeyed. To always allow discussion before they obey invites them to debate. A good motto to teach them is, *"Obey first. Ask questions later."*

---

[8] *Prov 26:4 Do not answer a fool according to his folly, or you will be like him yourself. 5 Answer a fool according to his folly, or he will be wise in his own eyes.*

—— 4 ——
Methods of Incorrect Discipline

"In the old days child guidance was something parents were expected to provide and not submit to."[1]

Before we look at the biblical approach to discipline in chapter 5, let us first consider a few unbiblical and fruitless methods of training children. I offer the following, with thanks to, Rick Fugate.[2]

EXAMPLES OF *INCORRECT* TRAINING

Methods that guarantee failure:

1. REPEATING INSTRUCTIONS AND MAKING THREATS

- Never give instructions more than once. If they have the ability to obey after the 3rd or the 100th time, they can obey the 1st time – *why not require it!*

- The child who habitually obeys after the 3rd time, has only done so with his parents' silent permission.

---

[1] 14,000 Quips & Quotes, E.C. McKenzie, Baker Book House
[2] Adapted in part from "What the Bible Says About Child Training," Family Building Seminars, 1996, J. Richard Fugate

You have accidentally trained him that way by not causing him to obey the first time.

Because you do not require obedience the first time you speak, your children must look for physical signs that tell them that you finally mean business:

- You raise your hand in a threatening manner.
- You go get the spanking paddle.
- Your voice gets harsh, your eyes narrow, and you use their middle name.
- You clench your jaw and pronounce your words slowly and precisely.
- Your voice gets so shrill, glass starts to shatter.
- Your face reaches a familiar shade of red, your eyes bug out, and you slur your words in low guttural sounds. *(The children may not even be certain which language you are speaking.)*
- That vein in your neck begins to pulsate.
- You fly into a rage and begin screaming, *"Now you've done it! Are you happy? You've pushed me over the edge!"*
- You use some catch phrase, such as:
    - *"I mean it!"*
    - *"Don't you look at me like that!"*
    - *"Do you want a spank?"*
    - *"All right! Now you're gonna get it!"*
    - *"Wait 'til your father gets home!"*
    - *"You keep that up and I'll give you something to cry about!"*

- *"If I have to come in there, you're really going to get it!"* or *"If I have to get up ...!"* or *"If I have to get out of bed ...!"*

- You know you are in the habit of repeating instructions if you hear yourself saying:
  - *"I've told you a hundred times..."*
  - *"How many times must I tell you...!"*
  - *"I'm not going to tell you again...!"*

  (Of course you are going to tell them again – you are telling them again right now! Besides, they know when they hear that threat, they still have 3 more before you act.)

Conditioning children to respond to harshness

Speaking harshly conditions our children to respond only to harshness. The very fact that they respond only to commands given in a harsh or stern tone, means that they know all other commands from us are not to be taken seriously. The parents who say, *"But they will only obey if I speak harshly,"* have accidentally created their own problem. Fortunately, we can recondition our children by giving all instructions calmly and one time.

Repeated instructions are *warnings*

Every time you repeat instructions you are giving warnings. With every warning your word becomes meaningless. If your word is meaningless, you've lost the respect necessary for successful training.

- Warnings make you an accomplice to their crimes. By not bringing immediate consequences, you are aiding and abetting them in their disobedience.

- Repeating instructions is a form of coddling which causes our children to grow dependent on us to remind them of their responsibilities. (Further discussion in chapter 7.)

Making threats

- Never threaten to spank. If your child is asserting his will against yours, causing you to want to warn him, he is already in need of chastisement. (Further discussion on chastisement in the next chapter.)

- Examples of making threats:
  - The obvious: *"If you don't do such and such, you're going to be in big trouble."*

  - *"Want me to get the spanking paddle? Here I go. (Stomp, stomp, stomp). Okay, I'm getting the paddle. Okay, I've got it and I'm coming in now to give you a spank if you've not obeyed yet. Okay?"*

  - Counting to 10 (or any number), ie:
  "1, 2, 3, 4, 5, 6, 7, 8, 8½, 9, 9½, 10. Wow, you juuuust made it."

  - Blatant lies. Typical: *"Okay, we're leaving without you. Bye, bye."* Outrageous: *"If you don't behave yourselves we will leave you here at Disneyland, and they will chain you into It's a Small World, and you'll be there forever. Where do you think they get all those kids to sing that song? They were naughty ones left behind by their parents."*

In case you missed it, let me repeat it: **Repeating commands and threatening children trains them to disobey.**

REMEMBER: We must not be angry at our children if they are not yet in the habit of obeying the first time we speak to them. Either they are young and we have not finished their training yet, or we have accidentally trained them to disobey, and it will require self-discipline on our parts to break our habit of repeating instructions. Either way, we must be patient – *they are still in training!*

2. BRIBING FOR OBEDIENCE

The difference between a bribe and a reward is that *bribes* are given to motivate behavior that should be mandatory. It is an effort by one *without* power to buy a favor from the one *with* power. *Rewards* are typically given to reinforce learned skills, good habits, or to give encouragement for the accomplishment of a non-moral task. *Moral* behavior may also be rewarded, but such rewards are not offered in advance because they would act as bribes for good behavior – they are best given without prior warning, and only occasionally.

- The parent who is unaware of his authority some-times resorts to offering bribes to his children to evoke obedience:

    - "We will pay you a dollar now and another one when we return, if we get a good report from the baby-sitter."

    - "If you behave in the grocery cart, I'll get you a treat when we check out."

    - "If you get into bed for your nap, I'll read your favorite story."

    - "You may have cake for dessert if you eat your vegetables first."

- "If you sit still and smile for the photographer, I'll buy you ice cream when we get done. So please sit still! It'll be Baskin–Robbins. Okay, honey?"

- Bribing children tells them:
  - that your word is insufficient motivation to obey.
  - that they are in charge and you are not.
  - that you are at their mercy.
  - that you are not worthy of their respect.

- Parents seeking to eliminate bribing from their training must be careful not to eliminate the reward of verbal praise and affirmation for good behavior.

Remember Solomon's wisdom: *"... a bribe corrupts the heart."*[1] We undermine our own efforts to shape our children's hearts if we corrupt them.

3. ALLOWING EXCUSES

Children must learn as a basic rule that there are no good reasons for disobedience (Except in case of emergency, of course.) When confronted with their defiance they should not be permitted to offer an excuse. If trained well, it might not even enter their minds to offer a justification.

- The parent who allows excuses for disobedience permits a child to avoid the consequences of his actions, inadvertently encouraging misbehavior.

- A child whose excuses are routinely accepted develops a "victim" mentality, eventually believing that nothing is ever his fault.

---

[1] Ecclesiastes 7:7

- Parents who do not want to think badly of their children may make up an excuse for them before they even investigate a problem, ie:

  - They get into trouble at school and you automatically believe their story that their teacher is out to get them.

  - Before they have a chance to offer an excuse, you presume their innocence and suggest to them an alibi.

- The parent who confronts a child for misbehavior and immediately asks, "Why did you do it?," sends the message that if a good enough reason can be offered, punishment may be avoided.

- A parent should first establish a child's guilt and have him accept responsibility, and then find out the reason why. *(Parents will need to determine if the action was intentional or accidental, so that they can set an appropriate consequence. Further discussion in the next chapter.)*

- Upon confrontation, a child should be permitted to respectfully state that his actions were of an emergency nature, ie:

  - "Yes, I pushed my sister, but she was about to be run over by a bike."

  - "Yes, I got out of bed, but little Jimmy's arm was caught in his crib."

  - "Yes, Dad, I interrupted you, and I am sorry for that, but Mom is out in the driveway, leaving in the car, and needs to know if you still want something at the store."

Parents accept excuses because . . .

- We put ourselves in our children's place, and know we would want mercy if it were us.

- We think we are too busy to stop and bring proper discipline.

- We are deceived about our children's nature and fall prey to their manipulation.

- We want to believe the best of our children, so are more than willing to allow them to cast the blame or shirk responsibility.

- We do not know who to believe in a dispute, and literally do not know what to do, so we accept an excuse and send the children off with just a warning.

- We hate conflict, and accepting an excuse is the easiest way to settle a problem.

- We are lazy, and choose our own comfort over our children's needs.

4. TRICKING OR MANIPULATING

Since the goal of child training is to help a child learn to subdue his self-will, parents must take every opportunity to subdue it when it manifests itself. Tricking a child may manipulate him into cooperating, but his will is not subdued in the process. One day he will be too smart to trick, and his parents will have on their hands a smart, strong-willed child, who resists their best parenting efforts.

Examples of tricking a child:

- When your authority is not sufficient to motivate your child to pick up their toys, you make a game of it, so that their desire for fun will gain their cooperation.

- When they will not obey your specific direction to go into their room for a nap, you become animated, playful, and silly, to make the walk to their room look like a lot of fun.

- When a child does not want to go outside to play, you give him 2 choices, ie: *"Do you want to walk outside or do you want me to carry you out?"* (He should be made to walk out under his own power in obedience to your word, and not tricked into compliance.)

- Instead of giving them a direct order to go to bed, manipulate them by saying, *"Which do you want to take with you to bed right now – the teddy bear or the doll?"*

- When they will not cooperate, you create a contest to gain compliance, ie: challenging them to get their room clean within a time limit. (This is not to discourage teaching them to set time limits for projects.)

5. DISTRACTING

Distracting children does not shape the will at all. It only diffuses the tension of the moment.

- Distracting may be a quick way to settle down a distraught or angry child, but it cannot be a substitute for discipline which will subdue the will. For example:

- A three year old who is throwing a fit, may forget that he was upset if an animated parent points out the window and exclaims, *"What could that be?"* However, the calming effect of the distraction does not subdue his will and should not be a substitute for chastisement.

- Angry children may be easily calmed by the offering of a toy or a treat in the midst of their distress, but that toy does not serve to subdue their will. It will, in fact, reward them for their behavior and encourage it in the future.

The only time distraction might be used is in a public setting where you are trapped in your seat and others are being disturbed by your child's anxiety, ie: On a plane, a bus, a submarine, etc. Whenever possible, an unruly child should be taken somewhere private and disciplined, where others will not be disturbed. The defense against being faced with such a situation is to train the child beforehand in the privacy of your home.

5

Nurturing Children With Discipline

"This hurts me more than it hurts you."
Famous parenting phrase probably first spoken by God
when He expelled Adam and Eve from the Garden.

One of the most painful aspects of parenting is the administering of discipline. When we were young, our parents told us, *"This hurts me more than it hurts you,"* but we didn't believe it – not until we became parents ourselves. Now we understand it – and we hate it – but we must do it!

The reason so many parents hate discipline is not just because they do not like to see their children cry, but because they are not 100% confident they are doing the right thing. Discipline is often stressful for them, because they are plagued by doubts, fears, and guilt.

Fortunately, God has given us in the Scriptures all the basic principles for determining when discipline is warranted and how to administer it. The parent who understands and applies these principles will find peace both in his heart and in his home.

WHAT IS GOD'S METHOD FOR DISCIPLINE?
Fathers, do not exasperate your children; instead, bring them up in the training and instruction of the Lord.   Ephesians 6:4

According to Ephesians 6:4, children are brought to maturity by TRAINING and INSTRUCTION in the Lord. The Greek word for TRAINING is paideia, which means *disciplinary education by correction, chastening, or punishment*. God's method for child TRAINING or "DISCIPLINARY EDUCATION" then involves elements of *correction, chastisement,* and *punishment*.

CORRECTION communicates the idea of *rectifying* something wrong, confronting a misbehaving child for the purpose of *making things right*. Correction is the foundation of TRAINING.

CHASTISEMENT communicates the idea of *making clean* by punishment with a rod. It is used in response to *rebellion*.

PUNISHMENT involves bringing natural consequences for misbehavior. It is used in response to *thoughtless disobedience*.

WHAT IS THE DIFFERENCE BETWEEN THOUGHT-LESS DISOBEDIENCE AND REBELLION?

Under Israelite Law, God distinguished two types of crimes – *intentional* and *accidental*. Each had a different penalty. For example, Numbers 35:11-28 tells us that if one man with malice aforethought murdered another, he was to be executed – life for life. However, if a man was irresponsible and killed another by accident, he was free to flee to a "city of refuge," where he and his family had to take up residence until the presiding high priest died. The willful murderer *intentionally*[1] violated the law, so suffered an equally severe physical consequence – death. The other *accidentally* violated the law, but still had to endure a consequence for his irresponsibility. Two different crimes – two proportionate penalties.

Biblical discipline of children follows the example God established in Jewish civil law. When a child *willfully* defies his parents and does wrong, he is in rebellion against their authority and must be chastised. If he disobeys them *thoughtlessly*, he is guilty of accidental misbehavior, and must receive a related consequence as a penalty.

The two types of misbehavior:

- Rebellion – willful disobedience
- Thoughtless disobedience

HOW DOES THE BIBLE SAY TO CHASTISE FOR REBELLION?

The Scriptures make it clear that chastisement is God's proper consequence for rebellion in children. Consider the following passage from Proverbs:

*Do not withhold chastisement from your children; if you **smite them with a rod**, they will not die. 14 If you **smite them with the rod**, you will save their souls from hell.*   Prov 23:13-14

God tells parents that they are not to withhold spankings from their children, for they help accomplish a soul-saving work.

---

[1] Num 35:20

The Hebrew word for smite is nakah, which means "to strike or swat." Parents are clearly instructed that they should train their children, spanking them on the bottom with the rod for chastisement.

It is important to note that according to the Scriptures, spankings are to be administered not with the *hand*, but with the *ROD*. The Hebrew word for ROD is shebet, which means a twig or switch. It is not a heavy implement that may bruise the skin, but a light one that will simply sting. The hand by itself is to be avoided, because it can cause bruising. Besides, those parents who use their hand will notice that their child will be unable to distinguish when he is being reached for in tenderness or in discipline – he will flinch whenever you reach for him.

Throughout the book of Proverbs, God emphasizes the value of the rod in firm discipline.

*Prov 22:15 Folly is bound up in the heart of a child, but **the rod of discipline will drive it** far from him.*

*Prov 29:15 The **rod of correction imparts wisdom**, but a child left to himself disgraces his mother.*

As we established in the introduction, the Hebrew words translated as "folly" or "foolishness" – keciyl and 'ivveleth – do not mean childish immaturity or silliness, but rather *deviousness, defiance,* and *rebellion*. The root meaning of keciyl is "fat," hence to be foolish is to be fat or "full of self." The rod is God's only means of subduing the self-will and rebellion that resides in every child. It is a quick, simple way of teaching obedience.

Chastisement is over quickly, the pain soon forgotten, but the impact is lasting. The negative consequence of pain conditions a child to say "No" to himself and thereby helping develop the self-discipline necessary for maturity.

"But I love my children too much to spank them"

*Prov 13:24 He who **spares the rod** hates his son, but he who loves him is careful to discipline him.*

*Prov 19:18 **Chasten thy son** while there is hope, and let not thy soul spare for his crying. (KJV)*

Spanking is not easy for most parents, because it brings grief to the very children they naturally want to comfort. Knowing the protective nature He gave us as parents, God warns that allowing soft feelings to inhibit spanking is tantamount to *hating* our children.[2] This only makes sense, since depriving children of what is good and necessary for their moral development, will be doing them harm. The problem is that some parents do not spank their children, because they want to spare *themselves* the heartache of watching their children cry, or because they fear their child's rejection.

It is not a healthy love that causes a parent to protect children from experiencing any discomfort or pain in life. In fact, it is often a self-serving love that makes parents refrain from spanking, or causes them

---

[2] Prov 13:24

to mete out soft disciplines and indulge their children. That kind of parental "kindness" is harmful.

For example, some children fear dentists. For them, just the thought of a dental appointment evokes panic. The overly compassionate parents, who succumb to their child's fears, harm him when they allow him to grow up without dental care. The same parents may exempt their child from eating "yuchy" foods like vegetables, and allow him to eat a steady diet of junk food. The Bible says that those parents actively "hate" their child by depriving him of what is good for him.

True compassion causes parents to ignore their own feelings of anguish at seeing their child's tears, and do what will be best for them in the long run. The parents who withhold the rod may do so out of a desire to spare *themselves* distress and avoid their child's rejection. Any parents who consistently spank their children will testify that it requires selfless love to die to themselves and do what is right for their children. Consider also Proverbs 3:11-12:

> *My son, despise not the chastening of the LORD; neither be weary of his correction: 12 For whom the LORD loveth he correcteth; even as a father the son in whom he delighteth. (KJV)*

God says that a father who loves and delights in his children will be faithful to discipline them. A significant evidence of God's love for us is His discipline. Consider also Hebrews 12:5-9:

> *And ye have forgotten the exhortation which speaketh unto you as unto children, My son, despise not thou the chastening of the Lord, nor*

*faint when thou art rebuked of him: 6 For **whom the Lord loveth he chasteneth**, and **scourgeth** [spanks] every son whom he receiveth. 7 If ye endure chastening, God dealeth with you as with sons; for what son is he whom the father chasteneth not? 8 But if ye be without chastisement, whereof all are partakers, then are ye bastards, and not sons. 9 Furthermore we have had fathers of our flesh which corrected us, and we gave them reverence: shall we not much rather be in subjection unto the Father of spirits, and live? (KJV)*

God says in verses 6-8 that the proof of parents' love is their willingness to spank their children, and that a child who is not spanked can hardly be called a son or daughter.

God in his love, has determined that suffering hardship is part of the maturing process for all believers,[3] we therefore can trust His brilliance when He tells us that our children learn self-discipline through the discipline imposed by spanking.

That society which does away with corporal punishment will raise undisciplined, self-consumed young people, who lack the security that comes from being required to stay within firm limits. Sweden and Denmark, famous for their prostitution, drugs, and child pornography, are the world's first countries to have outlawed spanking. Not surprisingly, since their first generation of undisciplined children has grown up, these two countries are now reported to have the

---

[3] Rom 5:3-5; Jam 1:2-4; Zech 13:9; 1 Pet 1:6-7; 4:1; Heb 12:7,10,11

highest teen suicide rates in the world. Eliminating the rod is not a sign of a civilized society, but of one in moral decline.

WHAT IS THE DIFFERENCE BETWEEN CHASTISEMENT AND CHILD ABUSE?

There is great fear today, among some parents that spanking of children is abusive, and causes emotional harm, or may breed violence. This concern is understandable, considering how we love our children. Fortunately, biblical chastisement bears good fruit, but unfortunately, not everyone follows God's guidelines. Consider the differences between loving, biblical chastisement and child abuse:

- *Chastisement* is a calm, controlled spanking on the bottom.
- *Abuse* is an angry, out-of-control beating, which may fall on the bottom or anywhere on the body. Such abusive chastisement may correct the misbehavior, but that child is not truly humbled – just terrorized into submission.

- *Chastisement* uses a lightweight rod on the bottom.
- *Abuse* shakes the body or pummels it with hands or any weapon handy.

- *Chastisement* is a planned action of love.
- *Abuse* is a reaction of anger. It is the venting of parental frustration, and feeds violence in children, causing them to vent their anger violently on others. *(Young ones raised with loving chastisement are typically the least violent among children, because they are self-restrained, are not ruled by*

their anger, and have been trained to behave
kindly toward all.)

- *Chastisement* is done after the first offense, while
  the parent is still calm.
- *Abuse* results when parents do not bring swift
  chastisement, but wait for the child's continued
  rebellion to make them angry enough to respond.
  Spanking is incorrectly used if it is a last resort
  rather than the first response for rebellion.

- *Chastisement* is loving and constructive.
- *Abuse* consists of hurtful, demeaning verbal attacks,
  which may accompany chastisement, but are often a
  substitute.

- *Chastisement* draws a parent and child together.
- *Abuse* alienates children from their parents.

HOW TO TELL WHEN A TIME OF DISCIPLINE IS COMPLETED

Many parents implement chastisement with their
children, but are frustrated, because it does not seem to
subdue their wills. The most common reason for this is
incomplete chastisement – it is administered as
discipline for rebellion, but is ended before its goals
have been accomplished.

What are the goals of chastisement?

1. To cause children to be humble before their
   parents' authority.

2. To cause them to take responsibility for what they
   have done.

3. To cause them to submit to the consequences of
   their actions.

Signs of unbroken rebellion after a time of chastisement:

- No obvious sign of brokenness or humility.
- Unwilling to admit fault and take responsibility for actions. Still blaming others or making excuses for misbehavior. Uses one of the defense mechanisms listed in chapter 8.
- Wallows in self-pity; maintains a "victim" mentality.
- Kicked or struggled the entire time of chastisement, never submitting to the discipline. *(Applies primarily to older children. Very young children may not hold still simply because they are not used to spankings.)*
- Refuses to hug the disciplining parent.
- Cries out for the non-disciplining parent; ie: If Daddy administers the discipline they might call for Mommy.
- Extended or extra loud crying (venting *anger* – not pain or sorrow).
- Blatantly angry: threatens to leave home, curses parent, sassy attitude, throws things, grumbles, storms around the house, etc.
- Tries to make parents feel guilty by sulking or pouting, or accusing them of improper discipline, ie: *"You spanked me in the wrong place."*
- Issues taunts like, *"You're mean,"* or *"I hate you,"* or *"That didn't hurt,"* or *"I can't wait 'til I'm old enough to move out!"*
- Expresses no remorse to God in prayer, and refuses to ask forgiveness of those they offended.

The chastisement is not over until a child is humble and has taken responsibility for his actions. It is only complete when his will is submitted to his parents. If after a time of chastisement, a child lacks proper humility, the chastisement obviously did not work, and should be repeated a second time. I rarely hear of any parent needing to administer a third set.[4]

Many parents battle strong-willed, defiant teenagers, because they never successfully completed a time of chastisement in the preadolescent years. Each incomplete time of chastisement served only to challenge, but not defeat their wills, making them stronger and stronger. By accident, some parents create super-strong-willed teens.

Parents who begin implementing chastisement when their children are toddlers, and properly complete each session, generally discover that their wills are completely subdued by the time they are 4 - 5 years old. Many testify that only occasional chastenings are required after that age.

BEHAVIOR DURING CHASTISEMENT THAT SHOULD <u>NOT</u> BE ALLOWED, AND MERITS EXTRA DISCIPLINE

It is important during chastisement that our children accept our authority and submit themselves to the

---

[4] Occasionally I do hear of a child who may not show his humility immediately after chastisement. Such a child, the parents tell me, finds humility when left alone to calm down for a few minutes following chastisement. If you try this approach, but yours does not settle down and become humble, then consider you are simply dealing with an exceptionally strong will which must be subdued through chastisement.

discipline we have determined they need. The following actions indicate resistance to your authority:

- Running away from you.
- Moving away from the rod.
- Kicking and struggling.
- Putting their hand in front of their bottom.
- Screaming at you.
- Pleading for mercy; making vehement promises of repentance.
- Requesting limited number of swats.
- Extra loud, angry crying.
- Lying; making excuses; trying to get out of trouble; casting blame.
- Guilt projection; threatening parent; accusing them of improper discipline.

HOW TO KNOW IT IS TIME TO CHASTISE

Any child who *knowingly or willfully disobeys* is in rebellion and needs chastisement.

Keep in mind that it is not the significant *effect* of the rebellious action that merits the rod – it is the rebellion itself, ie: It is not that they woke the baby up when they went into the off-limits room – it is the fact that they entered it in direct disobedience to your word. It is not the fact that they only took a crumb of cake after they were told not to touch it – it is that they intentionally disobeyed you.

CAUTION: Beware of trying to cure rebellion with "creative alternatives." Any alternative to chastisement is an alternative to *Scripture* – God offers no better solutions to subduing rebellion outside the Bible.

HOW TO IDENTIFY REBELLION[5]

A rebellious child is one . . .

- whose actions or attitude are in direct defiance of parental authority
- who asserts his will against the will of his parents
- who resists his parents' efforts to direct his life

Rebellion is manifested either *actively* or *passively*.

Active rebellion

1. Knowingly disobeying – *Active Rebellion*

- Willful, conscious disobedience to commands or established rules.

- Examples: *"Come here, Junior,"* and he doesn't budge. *"Stay in bed, Mary!"* and she gets up. *"Don't wear that, Terry!"* and she wears it.

2. Defiant verbal resistance – *Active Rebellion*

- Any form of sass or back-talk. (See chapter 9.)

- Intentions to disobey are announced by saying, "No!" Some offer a more blatantly disrespectful phrase of defiance, such as: *"Drop dead,"* *"Forget you,"* *"Get a life,"* or *"Whatever,"* etc.

- Will not accept parents' authority to make a decision. Refuses to take "No" for an answer.

- After receiving parent's decision, voices opinions relentlessly, even after instructed that the discussion is over.

- Fostered by parents who cave in to verbal resistance.

---

[5] Adapted, with additions, from Rick Fugate's, "What the Bible Says About Child Training."

3. Hitting parents – *Active Rebellion*

- Free vent is given to anger. Toddlers may slap, bite, or kick; older children may spit; teens may use their size and strength to cause serious injury.

4. Throwing temper tantrums – *Active Rebellion*

- Pitching a fit because their will has been thwarted.

- Toddlers may hold their breath, go stiff, go limp, cry uncontrollably, or fall down and pound their fists on the floor.

- Any age children may stomp their feet, scream, yell, throw or hit things, stare and glare, slam doors, etc.

5. Ignoring instructions – *Active Rebellion*

- After receiving parental instruction they continue to do as they please, as if they had never been spoken to.

- When receiving a tap under the table or a "look" from their parent that obviously says, "Knock it off," they look away or pretend they received no communication.

  (Parents blind to this form of rebellion will allow a child to not answer, perhaps even excusing their misbehavior as fatigue or mood.)

6. Resisting a parent-initiated action – *Active Rebellion*

- A parent chooses to initiate an action requiring their child's involvement, but the child refuses to cooperate.

- The child moves their shoulder away when a parent reaches out to touch or embrace him.

- Walking along, a parent reaches down and takes their child's hand and the child attempts to pull it away, perhaps continuing to tug until the parent lets go. (If the child is in pain because the blood in their hand has drained to their shoulder, and gangrene is setting in, they should be able to respectfully ask to have their hand back.)

- After being placed on their parent's lap, they attempt to get off. They should be permitted to respectfully ask to get down, but only after the parent is satisfied that they are willing to remain.

- While being held in their parent's arms a toddler struggles to get down.

- Goes limp or runs away when being ushered down the street.

- You reach for something in their hand and they hold onto it or pull it away. (They must be made to place the object in your hand. Do not grab or force from them something, unless it is a dangerous item, ie: knife, match, power tool, razor, etc.)

- After being placed in the highchair, a toddler arches his back and strains against the seat belt.

- Undoes something a parent has done, ie: turns the stereo volume back up after the parent has turned it down; turns a light back on after the parent has turned it off; retrieves something after parent has put it away.

Passive rebellion

Rebellion that is passive in expression tends to be

less conscious and premeditated than active rebellion. It is more of a rebellious *reaction* than a *planned* action. Those passively rebellious are often unaware of their defiance, requiring parents to work harder to expose to them their rebellion.

1. Consistent forgetfulness – *Passive rebellion*

   • Common to children is occasional forgetfulness. Consistent forgetfulness, however, is a form of rebellion.

   • When they can remember to set their alarm and dress themselves for soccer practice, but habitually forget to take out the garbage, they are demonstrating they can be capable when they choose to be. They just need greater motivation.

   • Remembers the entire prime time TV schedule, or never misses their favorite radio show, but always forgets to do their homework or make their bed.

   • They remember all that is important to them.

2. External obedience with a bad attitude – *Passive rebellion*

   • Obeys outwardly, but sends a defiant message: sulking, grumbling, whining, pouting, angry door slamming, glaring, silence, rough treatment of others or objects, etc.

   • They will obey, because they have to, but they will make you miserable.

   • They cooperate with your directions, but talk, complain, or whine about it the entire time, ie:

The three year old who lets his mother shower him, but is permitted to complain throughout the shower: *"But I don't want a shower. I don't want a shower."*

3. Obeying only on own terms – *Passive rebellion*

   • Does not come exactly when called; walks slowly.

   • Postpones obedience to show who's boss.

   • Does just one more after being told to stop.

   • Dictates to parent when they will obey: *"I'm getting a drink first,"* or *"I'll be there in a minute."*

4. Doing *what* is required, but not *how* it should be done – *Passive rebellion*

   • Does chores, but not by parents' established standards, ie: dishes are not quite clean, bed is not made properly, bedroom is not ordered as required.

   • You direct them to sit in their high chair and they squat.

   • Parents foster rebellion when they decide that rather than fight them, they will settle for partial obedience.

5. Walking away while being spoken to – *Passive rebellion*

   • Leaves the room while parent is in mid-sentence or during a pause between sentences.

- Keeps inching his way to the door before he's been dismissed. (Considered *passive* rebellion, because children are often unaware they are doing this.)

6. Lying to escape discipline – *Passive rebellion*

   - Premeditated lying is active rebellion, but reactively lying to escape discipline may be so unconsciously done that it qualifies as *passive*.

   - Many parents just expect their children to lie to get out of trouble, so neglect to chastise for it. It is important to chastise extra for this form of rebellion.

7. Violating unspoken, but understood rules – *Passive rebellion*

   - Although some rules are never spelled out, and some behaviors are never specifically prohibited, our children still know better. They intentionally disregard what they know will please you. What gives them away when they are caught, is behavior that suggests a violated conscience.

   - They must do some justifying in their minds, ie: Johnny takes Dad's power tool out of the garage to show his friends, knowing it would displease his parents, but justifies it to himself, saying, *"Dad lets me use it sometimes."* Yet, he jumps and hides the tool when Mom walks up to them.

   - Some children grant themselves permission to change an established house rule, because on one occasion their dad saw them violating it, but did not say anything. Their dad's inattention to what they were doing did not mean the rule had changed, and they know that, but they conveniently took his silence as permission.

- The toddler who is caught in the bathroom unrolling the toilet paper, may not have been specifically forbidden to unroll the tissue, but the tears he sheds, and the haste with which he continues his deed as he sees his mother approaching, verify that he knows he is doing wrong.

RESPONDING TO REBELLION WITH THREATS
The danger of threatening to spank

Children must learn early on that it is the authority of a parent's word that they must heed and that spankings will always be merited by willful defiance of that word. The parent who makes that clear to a young child and then proceeds throughout their childhood to regularly warn of each impending spank, accidentally sends the message that their word is not to be taken seriously. Their warnings may succeed in curtailing immediate misbehavior, but their child will learn to disrespect their word – and them.

Parents usually offer these warnings because they hope to correct rebellion without resorting to spanking. However, the child who is asserting his will against his parents is already in need of chastisement. The constant threats and reminders of impending spanks are blatant efforts to *persuade* a child to cease from misbehavior, and will not subdue the will.

THE CLEAR RULE: Tell a child a few times early in his life that he must be absolutely obedient to your word. After that, he must be held accountable to abide by all parental commands and should expect the pre-established consequences for violations, without further warnings.

HOW TO IDENTIFY THOUGHTLESS DISOBEDIENCE

Thoughtless disobedience. . .

- is any accidental violation of a rule or parental command.
- is not willful or defiant, nor is it planned or premeditated.
- is typically a thoughtless, impulsive, careless, or irresponsible action, or an honest mistake.[6]
- is an action that merits correction and a punitive consequence.

DISCIPLINE OF THOUGHTLESS DISOBEDIENCE

The most effective disciplines for acts of thoughtless disobedience are those in which the penalty is related to the crime. In this way the consequence reinforces the lesson that needs to be learned.

Less effective disciplines are those which have nothing to do with the misdeed, ie: When a child thoughtlessly leaves his bike out for the second time, what will teach him to be more responsible with his possessions? Will "grounding" him teach him to put his bike away? Will a "time out"? Sitting him in the corner? Fining him? Assigning him 10 pages of sentences?

---

[6] An honest mistake might be forgetting to carry out instructions or breaking a lamp.

None of these will be as effective as creating a consequence which relates directly to his failure.

The child who leaves his bike out has proven himself *irresponsible* with a personal possession – he needs to learn *responsibility*. A consequence that might teach him to be more responsible with his bike would be the loss of it for a time. Every time he wants to use it, but can't, he is reminded of his need to be more responsible with his bike. Plus, *he* – not Dad – will need to spend time removing the rust from the bike frame, which resulted from leaving the bike out in the evening dew.

A few typical **punishments** and principles to consider:

1. Loss of privileges. Parents must realize that most of what their children are allowed to do or to have is a *privilege* – not a *right*. Privileges should be revoked for those who prove themselves irresponsible. It is very important that the children be told in advance the possible discipline they will bring upon themselves.

   • Toys or clothes that are repeatedly left out may be taken away – permanently or for a period of time.

   • If older children are lazy or irresponsible in work, they repeat the chore, get extra jobs, or miss the next meal (2 Thes 3:10).

   • Declare to your children that they must complete their chores before they may leave for recreational outings. If it is time for them to leave for an outing, but you determine they were irresponsible,[7] so did not complete their chores, they must not be permitted to go until they are done. If a sports team has to compete without them,[8] they must learn the lesson that personal irresponsibility can hurt others. Most children who incur this kind of penalty rarely repeat the same irresponsibility a second time.

- If they are near the age for a driver's license, emphasize to them that driving is a privilege for those who prove themselves responsible. Postpone the date they may apply for their license by 1 month every time they manifest significant irresponsibility.

- If dinner is eaten too slowly or complained about, declare dinner over, take it away and give it to them for breakfast the next morning. *(Parents testify that this is one of the most effective disciplines they have ever tried.)*

- If they are unthankful for what is ordered for them at a restaurant, cancel their order and allow them only water to drink. *(Sounds harsh, but parents testify that after applying this discipline just once with one child, the others all learn and behave gratefully the rest of their lives. It is important they be forewarned of this penalty.)*

- If they nag or "push" you to do something for them, bringing it up after they have been

---

[7] Only if their uncompleted tasks were because of irresponsibility, and not because you gave them too much to do.

[8] If it is not the championship game.

instructed to drop the subject, they automatically lose it, even if you were already intending to give it to them.

- If they speak to you with disrespect, for a period of time they lose the privilege of speaking about what was on their mind.

2. Rectifying the damage done:

- Restitution – paying the cost of replacing items lost or broken. Children too young to have money should travel with you to the store and participate in the purchase of a replacement.

- Repair – repairing broken items. Children too young to make repairs should be with the one who does the work, so they can develop a sense of appreciation for the effects of their irresponsibility.

- Restoration – cleaning up any mess made – no matter how long it takes. Children too young to do it by themselves should be required to help in some way.

3. They must do a biblical research report on their problem area of sin, and create a plan for their own repentance.

4. Penalties should be increased in proportion to the number of offenses; repeated infractions should be treated as rebellion.

No discipline seems pleasant at the time, but painful. Later on, however, it produces a harvest of righteousness and peace for those who have been trained by it. Hebrews 12:11

——— 6 ———
What's Gone Wrong When Chastisement Doesn't Work?

"Many parents cannot subdue their child's will through chastisement, because they are busy strengthening it in other ways."

The first goal of child training is to subdue a child's self-will, and chastisement is God's primary means of accomplishing that goal. Many parents, however, find themselves unable to subdue their children's wills no matter how faithfully they administer chastisement. Their wills, in fact, seem to grow stronger every day. Such children not only continue in willful disobedience, but they manifest many of the traits of a self-indulgent child,[1] and the home bears the marks of a child-run home. Parents faced with this problem need to consider the possibility that although they practice chastisement as discipline, they are working against themselves by accidentally fostering self-indulgence and strengthening their children's wills in others ways. The following list offers various subtle ways parents inadvertently strengthen their children's sense of self-importance and send the message that their personal happiness is supreme.

---

[1] Chapter 2

HOW WE FOSTER SELF-INDULGENCE, STRENGTHEN THE WILL, CREATE A CHILD-RUN HOME AND KEEP OUR CHILDREN IMMATURE

To foster self-indulgence and strengthen the will . . .

1. Remove many of life's obstacles and exempt them from facing unpleasant circumstances.

- Resist the temptation to always grant children immediate gratification. It is important for them to learn to wait.

- Do not allow them to interrupt conversations. Permitting interruptions reinforces to them that they are the center of the universe and that what they want is of more importance than whatever anyone else is doing or speaking about.

- Do not drop everything and run to *them* when they call you. Rather, require them to come to you, unless it is an emergency.

- Do not jump to provide activity for them when they complain they are "bored." *(A good response to the child complaining of boredom is, "I'm glad to hear you are bored. You will find as you grow older that life is full of boring moments, so it is important for you to get used to enduring boredom now.")*

- Do not fear canceling plans for fun family events, just because you do not want your children to suffer the disappointment. Make or change plans according to what is wisest for everyone involved. Keep in mind that maturity is developed by learning to work through disappointments.

- If they complain about bread crusts, do not cut them off their sandwiches.

- Do not feed them every time they claim to be hungry. *(Children around the world learn to live daily with hunger pangs. Our children can certainly endure them for an hour. Although, most of the time, when a child complains of hunger, he is not hungry at all – he is really just bored.)*

- Require them to work daily around the house.

- When your guests have children younger than your children, require yours to get outside themselves, be friendly, and be hospitable hosts.

- Do not allow them sloppy work habits and messy rooms.

- Require them to pay their own bills in life and suffer the consequences for their choices.

To foster self-indulgence and strengthen the will . . .
2. Feed their appetite for pleasure.
   - Resist the compulsion to provide for them the pleasures you can afford. They must learn that they cannot have everything they want in life. Children who are never deprived of anything nice, grow up intolerant of life's trials.

   - Do not deprive them of fun, but do not feel the need to give them all the latest toys, fashionable clothes, etc.

   - Immaturity is fostered in children by gratifying all their desires for entertainment and spontaneous fun.

- Avoid giving them multiple opportunities for "escape," such as lots of TV, music, videotapes, comic books, and video games.

- Help them learn to phrase their requests, *"May I please?"* rather than, *"I want."*

- Do not give your toddler a readily available bag of snacks with which to walk around and munch on.

- Help them avoid the thinking that life is about leisure and recreation by not enrolling them in every sports and social program they desire.

To foster self-indulgence and strengthen the will . . .

3. Allow unrestrained self-expression and venting of passions.

- Do not permit them undisciplined communication. Require that they speak with self-restraint, ie: no whining, yelling, swearing, etc.

- Do not allow them to punish the family with their sulking and pouting.

- Permitting them to say anything they feel like saying reinforces to them that the expression of their feelings is more important than the feelings of those they might be speaking to.

- Discourage the "venting" of anger by permitting them to hit a pillow. *(Prohibiting them from taking their anger out on something will not make them victims of "repressed" emotions or warp their "psyche." It will teach them godliness. Children must learn that self-control and forgiveness are godly responses to anger.)*

- When they are upset, do not allow them to cry uncontrollably for as long as desired.

- Do not permit them to vent their destructive tendencies, ie: Don't hide the new magazines from toddlers, and give them old ones to tear up. *(They must learn to respect all property.)*

- Do not buy them washable crayons and permit them to color on the walls and furniture. You will not "suppress their creativity" by requiring them to color only on paper.

To foster self-indulgence and strengthen the will . . .
4. Allow them to influence family decisions when young.
   - Children develop humility and self-restraint by learning to cooperate with their parents' leadership. Those children who are granted a say in all decisions affecting the family, are sent the message that what they want is of equal or supreme importance as what their parents want for them.

   - Do not have frequent family votes. You may solicit input from your young children on occasion, but be careful of communicating to them that they have a *right* to a say in all family matters. The family is not a democracy, and children can learn selflessness by being required to accept their parents' decisions for them.

   - Guard against *always* letting them help decide which restaurant to choose; where to vacation; what type of music the family will listen to in the car; whether or not parents will go out for an evening; what the family will eat for dinner; which church to join, etc.

- Children must not be allowed to interrupt parental discussions, and offer their opinions without permission or invitation.

To foster self-indulgence and strengthen the will . . .

5. Allow them to make too many personal decisions too young.

   - Allowing young children to make "non-moral" decisions throughout their day seems harmless, but sends the message to them that they are in charge of themselves.

   - Typical non-moral choices that parents allow young children to make: What to wear; what to eat, when to eat; which cup to drink from, where they will sit at the table, which room to play in, which toys to play with, etc.

   - Do not *always* allow them to decide what they will order at restaurants. On occasion, exercise your parental prerogative of ordering for everyone.

   - Do not frequently allow them to do whatever they desire, ie: while Mom is shopping, Dad follows 3 year old Junior through the mall, permitting him to wander wherever he wants to go, giving him guidance only when in danger.

   - Children whose days are loosely structured and who make most of their own decisions, typically resist their parents' efforts to assert authority.

   - The child who has been in charge of himself all day, not surprisingly fights his parents' authority every night at bedtime.

To foster self-indulgence and strengthen the will . . .

6. Allow "substantial" compliance.

- When commands are clearly stated, and you settle for less than you requested, you teach them that you do not really expect them to obey, and you strengthen their resolve to pursue their own plans in the future.

- If you tell them to sit down in their high chair, but they squat instead, don't say, "*Close enough!*" and settle for less than what you requested.

- If you say, "*Put this away in your room,*" and you later find it dropped in their doorway, yet you do nothing about it, you reinforce their self-will.

- If you ask them to come to you, and they make a detour on the way, do not content yourself that they finally arrived. You must bring a consequence.

- If you say, "*Eat the rest of it,*" and they leave half of it, you must bring a consequence. Do not allow your exhaustion or fear of conflict to cause you to accept partial obedience, lest they be strengthened in their resolve to do the same next time.

- If you set a standard for a clean room, hold them to it, or you will find they "substantially comply" the rest of their lives.

- Obedience without humility is not true obedience, but is an expression of rebellion. If they obey, but with complaining and back talk, their wills remain strong.

- Children who are allowed to compromise parental commands, are being allowed to negotiate for a settlement. By no means are their wills subdued.

- If we allow our children to *substantially* comply with our commands, it may be that we dread conflict and want to avoid it, or we simply do not want to stop, and take the time and energy to chastise. Whatever the reason, our children are strengthened in their wills.

To foster self-indulgence and strengthen the will . . .
7. Engage in and then lose "will marathons."
   - Do not even start a will marathon. Give them a command and bring consequences if they disobey.

   - If you say, *"You will sit there until..."* and then cave in, you blatantly strengthen them.

   - If they sulk or whine and you finally give them what they want, you have rewarded them and have subtly strengthened their will.

   - If you hear yourself saying, *"I've told you 100 times tonight...! Oh, well, Go ahead..."* you know you have strengthened their wills.

To foster self-indulgence and strengthen the will . . .
8. Administer discipline inconsistently.
   - "Hit or miss" discipline encourages children to risk misbehavior. To a child, rules enforced haphazardly are like being given occasional permission.

   - The parents who do not work diligently to be consistent with rules and discipline strengthen

93

their children's wills. Their hope that their parents will forget, keeps their wills alive.

- Rules and consequences that are not written down are easily forgotten by child and parent. Write down your rules.

To foster self-indulgence and strengthen the will . . .
9. Allow selfishness to go unchecked.
   - Sharing is like all other biblical injunctions – we must require it of our children.

   - If you permit them to not share their possessions with friends or family, they grow in selfishness.

   - Allowing them a bad attitude when they do share keeps self-centeredness and selfishness alive.

   - Because there are times when possessions have special meaning, parents might make allowance for exceptions, ie:

     · A new gift has a 1-day "closed" period during which the recipient need not share it, but may if they desire.

     · Perhaps something of sentimental value or something they have been instructed to treat very carefully need not be shared.

     · A toy need not be shared with another child who has proven irresponsible in the past.

     · A bike or other "tool" may be exempted, because it has utilitarian value and it is important to minimize the chance of loss or damage.

   - Parents best teach selflessness by example.

To foster self-indulgence and strengthen the will . . .
10. Permit disrespect for others.
- Allowing them to be ruled by their whims, desires or curiosity, with little or no regard for others' possessions, privacy, or peace, breeds a strong self-interest.
- See chapter 9, "Raising Respectful Children."

To foster self-indulgence and strengthen the will . . .
11. Feed the ego.
- Do not reinforce their vanity. Do not place great importance on how impressively they must dress or groom themselves. Avoid talking a lot about their appearance.

- Guard against emphasizing *competitiveness* over *doing their best.* Giving winning a higher priority than glorifying God puts their eyes back on them.

- Do not overdo praise. Flattering children by constantly telling them how they are the best increases pride – not humility.

- Affirm them with "Pauline praise." In his epistles, the apostle Paul affirmed others' not by flattering them, but by thanking *God* for their godliness.[1] Drawing their attention back to God rather than to them will help maintain their humility.

To foster self-indulgence and strengthen the will . . .
12. Be abusive – both physically and emotionally.
- Attacks against children can create emotional

---

[1] Rom 1:8; 1 Cor 1:4-5; Phil 1:3; Col 1:3-5; 1 Thes 1:2-3; 2:13; 3:9; 2 Thes 1:3; 2:13

wounds that cause intense self-preoccupation and overwhelming concern for self-preservation.

- Abused children sometimes behave compliantly, but do so out of a strong commitment to self-protection, not a weak self-will. Their strong self-will may not surface until years later during marriage, when they crave, but fervently resist physical or emotional intimacy.

To foster self-indulgence and strengthen the will . . .
13. Reward defense mechanisms.
   - The parents who are fooled by their child's defense mechanisms will fail to cause their child to take responsibility for his actions, and thereby allow his will to remain unsubdued.

   - Discussed further in chapter 8, "How Children Avoid Personal Responsibility."

To foster self-indulgence and strengthen the will . . .
14. Allow them nonstop lobbying privileges.
   - Children allowed to push and nag their parents are exercising and strengthening their tenacity and determination for getting what they want.

   - The time and mental energy given to pursuing what they want fosters self-centeredness.

   - A child allowed unrestricted lobbying privileges misses a great opportunity to grow in self-restraint.

To foster self-indulgence and strengthen the will . . .
15. Justify all your instructions to your children.
   - Wise parents make their children wise by passing on to them the wise reasoning behind parental decisions. However, the parents who feel the

need to *justify* and prove the wisdom behind all instructions send the message to their child that they are accountable to him, and that he is owed an explanation.

- Such a child will perceive himself in charge of his parents and will be angered by their chastisement. *(See chapter 3, "Why children must learn to obey without knowing the reasons behind their parents' instructions.")*

To foster self-indulgence and strengthen the will . . .
16. Cease a time of chastisement before it succeeds.

- A child who is not required during chastisement to accept responsibility for what he had done, will not be humbled, and will perceive you as unfair.

- The parent who tries to bring humility to his child through chastisement, but does not succeed, only frustrates his child and strengthens his will more and more each session.

- See chapter 5, "How to Tell When a Time of Discipline is Completed."

To foster self-indulgence and strengthen the will . . .
17. Model a strong will.

- Children often learn willfulness by learning from their parents' example. Parents who refuse to submit to authority, whether God's or man's, teach their children that what *they* want is more important than what *others* want or need.

- The primary way children glean values, is not from their parents' instruction, but from watching what typically causes their parents anxiety.

- Parents who are self-indulgent, angry, or stubborn, should not be surprised to find themselves raising strong-willed children.

To foster self-indulgence and strengthen the will . . .
18. Be sure blessings are kept equal between children.
- Some parents try to keep family peace and minimize life's disappointments by being certain that each of their children receives the same gifts or good experiences enjoyed by their siblings, ie: When one child receives a gift from someone, the parent goes out and buys the others an equal gift. When one sibling is invited out by a friend, the parent insists that the others go along.

- By keeping all things equal we teach our children that they are *owed* blessings. Such children will feel deprived, and will tend to mope or wallow in self-pity, when they do not receive equal blessings as others.

- This fosters self-centeredness. Growing in love will require that they learn to rejoice for others.

To foster self-indulgence and strengthen the will . . .
19. Allow unchecked rebellion.
- Blindness to your child's rebellion allows it to fester and grow.
- See chapter 5, "How to Identify Rebellion."

This chapter lists only nineteen ways parents strengthen their children's wills, but there are many more. Wise parents will comb their parenting practices to discover how they might accidentally be hurting their own efforts to train their children.

7

Raising Responsible Children

"The child who is faithful and reliable in duties is well on his way to maturity."

In parenting, one of our goals is to raise children who accept responsibility for themselves and for their actions. We want them to be reliable and conscientious in their duties, and to be honest enough to admit their failures and weaknesses. Those children who grow up without learning responsibility are not prepared for adulthood, and will inevitably find themselves causing grief to all those who rely upon them.

Although loving parents will want their children to grow in personal responsibility, they may accidentally do much to hinder the process. In the name of "devotion" they protect their children from the consequences of their actions – they effectively *coddle* them. Children raised in this fashion grow up irresponsible and dependent on others to take care of them. When their children grow up, these parents are the ones who ask, *"Where did we go wrong? We did everything we could to give them a happy childhood."*

Is the answer obvious to you? Parents raise irresponsible or unappreciative children by *doing everything they can to make them happy.* In an attempt to give them a fulfilling childhood, they fail to give them the more significant experience of taking responsibility for themselves.

TIPS FOR TEACHING CHILDREN TO ASSUME RESPONSIBILITY FOR THEMSELVES

Do not do for your children that which they need to do for themselves.

- If they dirty something, they must clean it.

- If they leave a door open, they must go back and close it.

- If they leave something on, they must turn it off.

- If they leave a chore unfinished or poorly done, they must redo it until it is done properly. Do not do it for them no matter how much you fear it will not ever be done right.

- If they break something, they must pay for it. If they are too young to have money, they must assist their parent in its repair or attend the purchase of a new one. If an adolescent, give them a deadline for payment and don't lead them by the hand to find the means of earning the money. If you loan them the money because something must be repaired immediately, do not forget the debt or neglect to collect.

- If they are expected to pay for a new toy themselves, do not back down and make up the difference. Make them save a little longer.

- If they make an unwise business decision, or make a foolish purchase, let them live with their choices.

- If they are of driving age, but irresponsible in life, do not allow them the privilege of a driver's license.

- If they are in trouble at school or their behavior lands them in jail, make them live with the consequences of their actions. Don't bail them out.

- If they use illegal drugs, do not give them clean needles.

- If they are sexually promiscuous, do not give them birth control.

- If your daughter is pregnant, do not help her abort the child.

How to avoid coddling children

- Do not state for them, time after time, the established guidelines for chores and standards for behavior.

- Do not give them constant reminders to do their duties. It causes them to grow dependent on you to remember their responsibilities and inhibits the development of independence and self-reliance.

- Parents should be ready to follow through with every consequence or they should not propose them. Do not make empty threats, ie: *"If you're not ready, we're leaving you behind." "If you don't have it done, you're not going." "If you want to buy it, you must pay the entire amount." "If you complain about the food, you'll go without,"* etc.

- Do not wake them daily when they are old enough to set an alarm, or you will create dependence.

- When teens get up late and miss the bus to school, do not be too willing to drive them or write them an excuse if other transportation is available, such as a city bus or their feet. Let them be late.

- Do not give a teen last-minute lunch money or make an extra trip to school if they continually forget their lunch or do not allow time to make it. Let them fast.

- Do not do their homework assignments for them.

- Do not always give them a second chance when they continually fail to comply with standards, ie:

  - In an effort to get away with little work, their first efforts at cleaning their room are sloppy, but they know that all you will do is point out their mistakes and give them another chance. Why should they try their hardest the first time?

  - Their first effort at a math assignment is feeble, because they know you will simply point to their mistakes and give them another chance or two.

The fundamental principle is that a child should be held responsible to do everything he is capable of doing, as young as possible.

DETERMINING IF YOUR CHILDREN HAVE LEARNED RESPONSIBLE WORK HABITS

Signs of laziness:

- Expects each day to offer fun instead of work; great disappointment when wishes for recreation go unfulfilled.

- Avoids work: attempts to persuade parents that there is a better use for their time; offers excuses why they are unable to work; begs to have workload reduced.

- Avoids the task-assignor.
- Does as little as possible; works slowly.
- Puts off starting a job; chooses to play before work.
- Works inefficiently, ie: with one hand, sitting down, carries one at a time, etc.
- Does an incomplete job; quits before finished; jobs done sloppily with little attention to details.
- Negotiates with a sibling or friend to do the job.
- Looks for breaks; leaves the job early.
- Finds multiple excuses to stop work, ie: bathroom breaks, drinks, looking for tools, etc.
- Intentionally works slowly or does such an inadequate job that the parent takes over and finishes the task.
- Sleeps-in every opportunity; stays in bed after called.
- Works for "eye service;" only works hard when being supervised.
- Constant, unrelenting daydreaming.
- Disappears when thinks job is completed and neglects to ask if there is anything else to do.
- Chooses sedentary recreational activities. *(Not necessarily a sign of laziness, but can be a sign when considered with other signs.)*

DEVELOPING RESPONSIBILITY AND GOOD WORK HABITS

As most people make the transition from adolescence to adulthood, they discover that adulthood brings with it tremendous responsibilities. Many are unprepared for the demands of adult life, and never seem to "get the hang of it," so they fail miserably in careers, finances, and relationships. They were not prepared by their parents, so lack the maturity to successfully handle life. Do you want your children to grow up without maturity like so many who struggle today?

For centuries, parents understood that growing in maturity required children to learn while young, that life is about *responsibility* – not gratification and pleasure. Parents knew that the sooner children learned to be responsible, the sooner they matured. We need to implement that same principle with our children.

This idea is a foreign concept to many modern parents, who have grown up in affluent America. They believe that since children have only one childhood, it should be the most exciting and entertaining it can be. To them, childhood is not a preparation time for adulthood, but is a time of ease and freedom from responsibility. Instead of teaching children to do as much as they can as early as they can, they encourage them in self-gratification well into their teen years. These parents misunderstand parental nurturing, and coddle their children long after they are capable of caring for themselves and serving others. To them the very suggestion that children should preoccupy themselves with learning to be *responsible* and not with *play* is offensive. If that is you, please reconsider.

If we are overindulgent parents, having as our highest goal to give our children fun, fulfilling childhoods, our children will learn to equate joy with *fun*. They must learn, however, that the greatest joy comes not through abundant recreation, but through a job well-done, and more specifically, through serving others.[1] **If you desire for your children a fulfilling childhood and a satisfying life, then teach them responsibility by teaching them to love[2] and serve others**.[3] (Further discussion in chapter 15.)

---

[1] John 15:10-12
[2] John 13:34; 15:12; 1 John 3:23; 2:8-11; 4:21; 2 John 1:5-6; 1 Cor 9:21; Rom 13:8-10; Jam 2:8
[3] Gal 5:13-14; John 13:14-15; Gal 6:2, 1 John 3:16; Eph 5:2; Rom 12:10

8

How Children Avoid Personal Responsibility

"The 10 year old child who accepts personal responsibility has greater maturity in many ways than the 50 year old adult who blames others."

One of the key ingredients to maturity is the ability to take responsibility for oneself and one's actions. Our discipline of our children, therefore, becomes useless, and even harmful, if we carry it out, but fail to cause them to accept responsibility for their misbehavior. In order to help our children take responsibility for themselves, we must be aware of the methods and tactics that can be used to fool us. The following list is not taken from a psychology textbook, but is simply the result of years of cataloging the methods of avoidance used by most people – children and adults alike. As you study through the list evaluating your children's behavior, don't be fooled by your own defense mechanisms and miss the application in your own life.

HOW DO CHILDREN AVOID TAKING PERSONAL RESPONSIBILITY FOR BEHAVIOR?

1. **Denial** – a willful refusal to even *consider* their contribution to a problem; a dangerous form of *self*

deceit that fosters lying. Denial says, *"It's never my fault."* Some level of denial is at the root of most defense mechanisms.

2. **Rationalization** – avoiding taking full responsibility for behavior by means of excuse and self-justification. Those with this propensity to rationalize their behavior often deceive themselves with extensive reasoning, and feel misunderstood.

3. **Partial confession** – acknowledging that something bad has happened, but stating it in a way which ignores or avoids their responsibility, ie: *"The lamp broke,"* rather than, *"I broke the lamp."* It is VERY important in confronting our children that we teach them to assume responsibility for themselves by making clear confessions of their mistakes or sins.

4. **Discreditation** – ignoring their parent's confrontation by discrediting them in their own minds through faultfinding, ie: *"You criticize me for that? Well, who are you to talk!? You do the same thing."* Often this is learned by watching their parents do it with each other.

5. **Guilt projection** – disavowing personal responsibility by casting the blame onto someone or something else. Adam first did it – blaming God for giving him Eve.[1] Children who hold others responsible for their own mistakes and failures may develop the "everyone owes me" mentality, ie: *"I'm never responsible for anything*

---

[1] Gen 3:12

wrong in my life. It's always someone else's fault." Those who feel the world is in debt to them may employ some method of **"emotional manipulation"** to make others feel guilty or responsible for their difficult situation. They may even have the audacity to become angry with those who fail to take responsibility for them, and are rarely satisfied with undeserved help they receive. They are often unappreciative for favors given them.

6. ***Guilt sharing*** – accepting blame, but implicating as many others as possible in the crime. The more others are made to look guilty the less spotlight on the one caught – he is just one of many. Those who confess for others also may hope to be held less responsible, or be dealt with more leniently, because they have been so cooperative.

7. ***Avoidance*** – staying away from their parents or others who may confront them about their behavior, ie: may come home late from school, find excuses to stay at friend's house, begs to change churches, etc.

8. ***Minimizing*** – acknowledging personal responsibility, but downplaying the significance or seriousness of the crime, ie: *"Yes, but what I did really wasn't that bad."*

9. ***Emotional Manipulation*** – a child's attempt to control a parent by manipulating their most vulnerable emotions and insecurities.

a. **withdrawal** – By retreating into himself or giving off the "silent treatment," a child will attempt to punish and manipulate his parents with guilt. Sulking and pouting are plain attempts to control his parents and influence their exercise of discipline.

b. **charm** – Those children who learn that they are "cute" can resort to playing up their "cuteness" to soften their parents' anger. This cuteness includes well-timed expressions of affection. Many an unwary parent has helped their child learn to escape responsibility by falling victim to charm.

c. **whining** – Many children learn to manipulate a parent by wearing them down emotionally with constant whining. Parents finally succumb to the will of the child, giving in to the whining as they would to torture.

d. **emotional outbursts** – By an intense outburst of crying a child can manipulate a parent in 2 ways:

1.) Tears can evoke compassion and guilt in the parent and halt further confrontation. Attention then becomes focused on the *"hurt"* and *"distressed"* condition of the crying child. A parent can even be manipulated into an apology when this technique is used properly.

2.) Tears can fool the conviction-resisting child themselves. They become so preoccupied with their "distress" that they will no longer focus on their responsibility. For many this form of self-

pity is a standard defense mechanism that, if not broken by parents, solidifies in the child an inability to hear correction or reproof as adults.

e. **departure** – In an attempt to play on the their parents' insecurities, they will suddenly storm out of a conversation or run to their room. They are playing the games, *"If you really love me you will follow,"* or possibly, *"You've really done it now – I'm hurt!"* Again, if successful, they can evoke an apology. (A parent should also consider that despite the disrespectful departure, their child might have been genuinely hurt.)

f. **intimidation** – A child who subconsciously perceives himself as in control of his home will be furious that his parents have had the audacity to thwart his will. By throwing a tantrum, blowing up into a rage, or by maintaining an irritable mood, a child can unnerve an insecure parent. Fearing the loss of their child's approval they may compromise the exercise of their authority, inadvertently preserving their child's control of their home. A child's anger may also intimidate those who simply dislike *conflict* or those who mistakenly think they have pushed their child to the point of exasperation.

g. **patronization** – Because some children hate tension or conflict they become agreeable to everything said by their parent. Although they do not believe what they are agreeing to, they are accommodating to appease their parent, thereby diffusing the tension, and bringing to a close the time of confrontation. A child doing this may often leave angry, and feeling unjustly accused.

h. *false humility* – In the midst of confrontation a child might acknowledge his guilt, but overstate it with the intent of evoking compassion and mercy in his parents. His self-depreciation may even cause his parents to minimize the sin, saying something like, *"Don't be so hard on yourself. You're not that bad."*

i. *penance* – They do something good to make up for doing something wrong, so they will not have to humble themselves to ask forgiveness, ie: they pick you flowers, draw you a picture, cuddle with you, etc. Keep in mind that these manipulative acts of "affection" are done in *place* of taking responsibility for a wrongdoing, and are not to be confused with genuine acts of affection that might accompany confession and repentance.

10. *Redirection* – directing a conversation away from himself by changing the subject. The following are typical means of *redirection* a child might use to take the attention off of himself:

a. *accusation* – He will find fault with his parent. If he can get his parents on the defensive by pointing out their failures he will take the heat off himself and focus the attention on them. It may also be an effective means of guilt projection and emotional manipulation.

b. *flattery* – He will stroke his parents with the intent of getting them more concerned about themselves than him. This buttering up of their ego may also cause them to lighten their discipline on him, since he has now made them feel good about themselves.

c. **embarrassment** – By making a scene in a public place many children successfully change the focus of a conversation. This is commonly done with an emotional outburst involving anger, crying, or a raised voice.

d. **division** – "Divide and conquer" is the concept behind this one. If a child can play one parent against the other he can divert their attention to a power struggle between them, thereby potentially weakening the discipline he faces.

e. **diversion** – A simple diversion to a completely unrelated subject; accomplished by either bringing up a new subject or by asking an unrelated question. This includes intentionally misinterpreting something which has been said and going into great detail addressing an unrelated topic.

f. **false confession** – When the parents are probing too closely to the root cause of their adolescent child's personal problem, he may make a false confession. By acknowledging an unrelated or more socially acceptable sin than the one he knows he is actually guilty of, he keeps his parents off track, and can continue in his ways. His confession may even impress them as *humility*.

11. **Exemption** – Many children discover early in their lives that a debilitation or "handicap" exempts them from complete responsibility for their actions. Not many children are aware that feeling sorry for oneself fuels self-exemption, because the very nature of self-pity is to blind. They may even learn to welcome debilitations or to create problems for themselves that cause others to become more tolerant and understanding of their misbehavior.

a. **sickness** – Some children find such solace in the tolerance shown them during an illness that they convince themselves they are sick much the time. If their parents or others do not sufficiently exempt them from their responsibilities then they wallow in self-pity, believing that they are being unfairly treated. If this pattern of self-exemption is not stopped while they are young, by the time they reach adulthood they will be victim to one psychosomatic disorder after another.

b. **fatigue, hunger, and irritability** – Many parents excuse their children's misbehavior if the hour is late or if they have missed a nap. This reinforces to the child that they needn't always exercise self-control. Those who have heard their parents announce the "reason" for their misbehavior may even learn to feign sleepiness or hunger as an excuse. Parents may be amazed to discover that a fussy child can exercise self-control if required.

c. **physical injury** – We properly respond with compassion and expect less "action" from children beset by an injury. Many children however, learn to make the most of injuries, no matter how minor, to gain exemption from their responsibilities in life. This ploy is especially effective for a child seeking to escape accountability for his part in a conflict with another child. Parents, take note – when you pick up your little one to confront him on misbehavior, does he suddenly assume a pitiful expression on his face, point to an old scab or scar on his leg, and say, "I hurt myself"?

d. **emotional injury** – In the same way that those with physical injuries exempt themselves from physical activities, those who perceive themselves as victims of "emotional injuries" may exempt themselves from their roles and responsibilities, both spiritual and social. As real as the pain is from emotional wounds, Jesus tells us that we are not to maintain anger or bitterness against those who hurt us. Bitterness and unforgiveness may never be excused with the phrase, *"I'm just hurt."* Anticipating his people would not be exempted from the physical and emotional abuse in this world, Christ commanded that we love, bless, and pray for those who hurt us. We are always called to love and forgive as Christ loved and forgave His persecutors. We must teach our children that they are not exempted. (One tip – before speaking to the child about the need to forgive, be sure to express compassion for them first. [Rom 12:15])

e. ***rejection*** – One of the most difficult sights for a parent to see is his child crying because of rejection of his peers. Parental comfort is a powerful and appropriate balm to that child's ailing heart. However, some children are very self-centered and have a difficult time developing relationships. Parents must be careful to not exempt their self-centered children from learning the selflessness required of friendships. That child who is allowed to wallow in rejection and self-pity, and is not trained to take responsibility for himself, will always lack social maturity and may eventually develop a subtle type of persecution complex.

f. ***shyness*** – Though some children are more introverted than others, many learn to use their "shyness" as an excuse to be exempted from stressful social situations, ie: They offer silence in response to an adult's greeting or hide behind your leg; they insist that you call a store for them when they have a question; they refuse to apologize for a wrong they have done to another. A child may have a quiet personality, but shyness is no excuse for poor manners and subsequent hurt feelings. A refusal to be polite is a matter of will. Children as well as adults, when faced with any unpleasant task, must put aside their own personal comfort and do what is loving toward others.[2]

g. ***labels*** – Many children are born with or develop physical disabilities or chemical imbalances that

---

[2] Phil 2:3

affect the control they have over themselves. These handicaps may include learning disabilities, Attention Deficit Hyperactive Disorder, autism, etc. As real and disabling as these conditions are, some children learn to use their "label" to their advantage. They hear their parents excuse their misbehavior to others, so they misbehave knowing that their "condition" exempts them from the standards of behavior expected of others. When they have been disobedient or unruly they may tell others things like, *"Well, I'm A.D.D. you know,"* or *"I'm a little wild today, because I didn't have my pill this morning."*

12. **Selective hearing** – hearing or remembering only what they want to hear. Although a discussion, confrontation, or words of advice may be clearly spoken, some children may glean only the words or phrases that are *useful* to them. They may twist phrases or take words out of context to later justify misbehavior, conveniently blaming their parent for their actions. Listening selectively means that after a reconciliation session with his sister, Johnny may recall only that which applies to her. He may "mishear" and then misstate what was said because he wants an excuse to disregard the confrontation. He may even misconstrue the truth as an excuse for his reaction of self-pity or emotional outbursts, ie: sulking, tears, rage, etc.

13. **Blocking** – a firm, resistant denial of what is being said, related to selective hearing. The child in this case refuses to hear or consider anything contrary to

their beliefs or practices. Either their mind is made up or their heart is so hardened that they cannot even begin to consider what is offered them. Those who "block" respond to confrontation as if they didn't hear it. They tune it out. Too much is at stake for them. Acknowledging the validity of what is said will require them to change, and they do not want to. Subconsciously, they may agree with their parent, but they will not admit it lest they feel guilt.

14. **Self-pity** – feeling sorry for oneself excuses one from personal responsibility by concentrating attention on one's "oppressed" and "victimized" condition. Those children using self-pity consume themselves with the hurt from "unfair" treatment they have received. Not uncommonly, they are bitter and unforgiving towards those they hold responsible. One using self-pity as a defense mechanism feels "picked on" and is prone to sulking, pouting, and whining to solicit pity. Frequently, they will tell their "story" to anyone who will listen, just to garner sympathy or support for their side. Self-pity can be a strong factor in **denial, guilt projection, rationalization, emotional manipulation, redirection, selective hearing,** and **exemption.** Ultimately, the self-pitying child rarely solicits pity by appealing directly to others, but their manner seems to say, *"Aren't I pitiful – I am so un-responsible for what has happened to me – I am such a victim of others – don't you just feel sorry for me."* Parents duped by self-pity will withhold needed correction, because they feel sorry for their child.

A WORD OF CAUTION

The parents who are freshly aware of their children's methods for escaping responsibility may be tempted to become suspicious of everything their children do. Every tear, every hurt, and every appeal for sympathy may possibly now be regarded with mistrust.

Parents, be careful of allowing your new knowledge to overshadow your natural compassion. Watch yourself. Do you hear yourself thinking things like, *"You're not going to fool me, kid. I'm onto your game."* If so, then you are out of balance, and you may begin to exasperate your child.

Remember – Jesus told us to be as "wise as serpents, and as harmless as doves,"[3] but he also told us that love "hopes all things."[4] Do not be fooled by your children, but do not automatically think the worst of them either.

If you discern your child is using one of these methods of avoiding personal responsibility, the goal is not for you to simply recognize it, but to train your child to be aware of it and turn away from it. You want them to learn to become honest with themselves and others.

---

[3] Matt 10:16
[4] 1 Cor 13:7

9

Raising Respectful Children

Children, obey your parents in the Lord, for this is right. 2 "Honor your father and mother"- which is the first commandment with a promise, 3 "that it may go well with you and that you may enjoy long life on the earth." Ephesians 6:1-3

WHY IS IT IMPORTANT FOR CHILDREN TO LEARN TO RESPECT ADULT AUTHORITY?

The Bible commands not only that children respect their parents, but like adults, they must give honor to whomever honor is due.[1] They are to behave respectfully toward all those in authority, whether it is a schoolteacher, a baby-sitter, a governing official,[2] a police officer,[3] a church leader,[4] or just someone older.[5] It is important that children learn to respect all adult authority for several reasons:

- Learning to honor adult authority when young prepares a child for future adult responsibilities in areas of work, social relationships, and citizenship.

---

[1] Rom 13:7; 1 Pet 2:17
[2] 1 Pet 2:13-14
[3] Rom 13:1-5
[4] Heb 13:17
[5] Lev 19:32; 1 Tim 5:1; Job 12:12

- Being required to behave and communicate respectfully teaches a child self-restraint and reinforces to them that not everything they feel or think need be expressed.

- Learning to honor adult authority when young prepares a child to respect God's authority.

WHAT IS RESPECT?

Hebrew

kabad, kaw-bad'; literally - to be weighty, i.e. to take seriously; to regard with sobriety

yare', yaw-ray'; to fear; to be frightened of; ie: to revere or treat with reverence

Greek

timao, tim-ah'-o; to esteem and place great value upon; to revere; to show honor

phobos, fob'-os; to regard with fear or fright

WHAT DOES IT MEAN TO SHOW RESPECT FOR AUTHORITY?

Based on the Greek and Hebrew word meanings, there are 2 elements of **RESPECT**:

1. To treat those in authority with the realization that they have power in your life. It means that when they speak, you listen and obey them, fearing the consequences they could bring for disrespect.

2. To behave in a way which shows value to the one deserving of honor. Most significantly, respect is more a *behavior* than it is a *feeling*.

Conversely, **DISRESPECT** is showing disregard or contempt for authority; communicating little regard for the office or station in life of another. It is treating parents or any adult with the familiarity appropriate a peer.

EXAMPLES OF DISRESPECT TOWARD ADULTS

Defiant Attitude

1. Knowingly disobeying direct commands or wishes; ie: active or passive rebellion.

2. Threatening statements such as, *"I can't wait until I'm old enough to move out of here!"*

3. Rude, intentionally hurtful remarks such as, *"I hate you."*

4. Grumbling about any parental decision qualifies as disrespect. Objections such as, *"That's a dumb idea,"* are insulting. Threats such as, *"I'm going to have a rotten time,"* are not only impolite and ungrateful, but attempt to manipulate a parent.

5. Speaking in an irreverent manner such as with sarcasm or a voice raised in anger.

6. Storming out of the house, slamming doors, etc.

7. Defiant statements such as, *"I'll do it when I get around to it,"* or responses such as: *"Yeah, yeah, yeah." "Hold your shirt on." "Whatever!" "Don't have a cow."*

8. Trying to show they are unfazed by discipline; accepting it casually – an attitude of "no big deal"

Inappropriate Familiarity

1. Scripture indicates that children are not the social equals of adults, and therefore should not be allowed to treat them as peers. We are to treat others with honor in respect for their age and station in life, ie:

   - *Rise in the presence of the aged, show respect for the elderly and revere your God. I am the LORD. Leviticus 19:32[1]*

   - *Do not rebuke an older man harshly, but exhort him as if he were your father. Treat younger men as brothers, 2 older women as mothers, and younger women as sisters, with absolute purity. 1 Timothy 5:1-2*

   - *Show proper respect to everyone: Love the brotherhood of believers, fear God, honor the king. 1 Pet 2:17*

   As indicated by the following passages that describe degenerating societies, one sign of a family in trouble is disrespect for parents and the elderly:

   - *The people will be oppressed, everyone by another and everyone by a neighbor; the youth will be insolent to the elder, and the base to the honorable. Isa 3:5 (NRSV)*

   - *Princes have been hung up by their hands; elders are shown no respect. Lam 5:12*

   - *"Brother will betray brother to death, and a father his child. Children will rebel against*

---

[1] God regards respect for the elderly as part of our worship of Him. See also Prov 16:31; 20:29; Job 32:4-6

> *their parents and have them put to death.*
> Mark 13:12

2. Allowing children to call adults by their first name grants them peer-level status, and shows no honor for their station in life.

   Physicians are addressed as "Doctor" by their patients, but are on a first-name basis with their peers. In the military, higher-ranking officers are addressed as "Sir" by those under their command, but are on a first-name basis with their fellow officers. Many schools have found that those teachers who allow students to address them on a first name basis, may be *popular* with the students, but are often less *respected* by them.

   Children are not the peers of adults, and therefore should be required to address them with respectful titles, ie: Mr. & Mrs., Aunt & Uncle, Pastor, Sir, Ma'am, etc.

3. Calling parents derogatory names is disrespectful, no matter how innocent sounding, or how playful the context, ie: *"Dad, you dummy!"*

4. Taunting or teasing communicates disrespect. If teasing is unacceptable towards children, it is even less appropriate towards parents, ie: *When you ask for them to pass the butter, they hold it out to you, but just out of your reach.*

5. Giving orders, even playful ones, such as, *"Say, `please'"* is inappropriate and unacceptable.

6. Children who yell for parents to come to *them,* rather than going to the parents, show no regard for the importance of what their parents might be

doing. In recognizing the Father's greater position, Jesus once said, *"... I am going to the Father, for the Father is greater than I."*[2] It is appropriate for children to call for their parents to come to them in emergency situations, but not to look at a plaything they constructed.

7. Snide looks, rolling of the eyes, mockery or teasing of adults; comments like: *"Ha, ha, so funny I forgot to laugh,"* might be tolerable banter with peers, but are too familiar with those worthy of respect. Dad's jokes may be corny, but he may not be mocked for them.

8. Unless it is an emergency, children should never be permitted to criticize those over them in authority, make fun of their failures, or correct them without first securing their permission, ie: If you are telling your spouse about an incident that happened last week, when your child interrupts your conversation to declare that the incident happened not last week, but 2 weeks ago, they are correcting you and should reap a disciplinary consequence.

9. Children should not permitted to "bad mouth" any adults, even those whose behavior may be severely wrong, or those you may deem worthy of disrespect, ie: absentee father, hostile neighbor, anti-family politician, etc.

Concern for SELF Over Others

1. Ungratefulness shown for a gift given them – shows contempt and disrespect for the feelings of the

---

[2] John 14:28; 13:16

giver. Children must learn that the feelings of the giver are more important than the satisfaction of the recipient.

2. Complaining about what has been given them for dinner or what has been ordered for them at a restaurant – is impolite and ungrateful.

3. Silence in response to an adult's greeting – is impolite. Shyness is no excuse for bad manners and hurt feelings. A refusal to be polite is a matter of will. *(Even though it is not comfortable for them to meet someone new, they must not be permitted to refuse to be polite, and greet them.)*

4. Interrupting adult conversations when not an emergency shows they think that what is on their mind is more important than what others are doing or are talking about. They must be trained to consider the impact of all their actions on others.

5. Disturbing others in public shows a preoccupation with personal pleasure and a lack of consideration for others' privacy or peace, ie: playing in a store, excessive noise, running in a mall, playing a portable stereo loudly at the beach, etc.

6. Taking the best seat, and releasing it to an adult or a guest, only under coercion, shows a concern for personal comfort over others.

Giving Sass or back-talk

1. Sass is any response to an adult statement that is given without *permission* or *invitation,* ie:

   • Denying responsibility

- Questioning or challenging

- Offering unsolicited explanations during correction.

- Grumbling or blurting out objections about parental decisions.

2. Contradicting a parent's statement is the same as calling them a liar. If a child believes his parent is mistaken about something, then he should be allowed to offer his opinion, but only after he has secured his parents' permission to do so.

3. If you allow them to continue to sass throughout childhood, they will make themselves obnoxious to their future employers and will limit their success in social relationships as well. Sass is a form of defiance and reveals a lack of submission to authority.

4. Sass is any response except, *"Yes, Dad," "Yes, Mom," "May I appeal?"* or some other respectful request for permission for further discussion.

RESPECTFUL RESPONSES TO PARENTAL INSTRUCTIONS

Respectful responses are ones that indicate humble subjection to authority, such as:

- *"Yes, Dad"*
- *"Sure, Mom"*

Children should be able to make appeals for discussion, but only if they show respectful subjection to authority, and first secure permission before offering their questions or thoughts. Possible appeals:

- *"May I appeal?"*

- *"May I have your permission to discuss this?"*
- *"Excuse me, Dad, may I offer you new information before you decide?"*
- *"May I inquire as to your reasoning?"*

Whatever the appeal process we give our children, they should never be permitted to respond with "sass" or "back-talk." If they respond argumentatively, or with anything other than a pre-established respectful response, then we must guard ourselves from responding to them with anything except correction. To answer them or continue in dialogue is to reward them and encourage future sass. Those children who abuse the appeal privilege by appealing every instruction, should have it revoked for a time.

TEACHING RESPECT FOR OTHERS AND THEIR BELONGINGS BY REQUIRING CHILDREN TO ASK PERMISSION

In the military a soldier shows his respect by requesting permission to speak before offering his ideas or asking questions. In business a wise worker asks permission of his boss before taking a vacation. In court attorneys do not tell the presiding judge what to do, but humbly make requests. Asking permission is an important demonstration of respect for others and acknowledgment of their authority. A child who does not ask permission, but presumes to proceed with his own plans, is exercising authority he has not been given. He is demonstrating a "respect" for his own interests over the interests of another. It is imperative that children learn to show respect for others by asking permission. The following are typical situations in which asking permission would be appropriate:

- They touch or pick up something which belongs to another: ie: *toys at the home of a friend; mail on the kitchen table; a freshly glued piece of china drying on the counter; a mouse trap behind the dryer; the refrigerator handle, Dad's tools, etc.*

Respectful approach: *"May I play with this toy? May I touch this? May I eat this?"*

- In response to instructions they ask "Why?" without first securing your permission.

Respectful approach: *"May I have your permission to ask why?; May I appeal?"*

- After receiving instructions or correction, they walk away from you before being formally dismissed.

Respectful approach: *"Is there anything else? May I go now?'*

- Going off to play after deciding they have completed enough of their chores.

Respectful approach: *"Mom, I've finished my chores, is there anything else you need me to do, or may I go off to play now?"*

- They overhear a parental conversation and offer their opinion when they have not been invited.

Respectful approach: *"May I offer my vote on where we go out to dinner tonight?; Would you be open to hearing where the kids' would like to vacation this year?"*

- *Telling* you rather than *asking* you things; ie *"I'm going next-door to play; I'm going to spend the night at So & So's house this Friday; I'm going to get a cookie; I'm not going back to that school!"*

  Respectful approach: *"May I go next-door to play?; May I have something to eat?"*

- Responding to instructions with statements rather than with questions, ie: *"I'm not going to bed that early; I'll be there in a minute – I'm getting a drink first; But I don't want to...!"*

  Respectful approach: *"May I stay up later? May I get a drink first? May I offer you my ideas?"*

The general rule for our children: *If you have not been granted authority, do not make decisions on your own. If it does not belong to you, do not touch it. If you have not secured permission, do not offer your opinion.*

SHOULD CHILDREN BE ALLOWED TO BE VULGAR?

Vulgarity shows no respect for others, for oneself, or for that which is private or sacred. Scripture forbids vulgarity and commands us to not allow unwholesome, unedifying speech to come out of our mouths.

> *Eph 5:4 Nor should there be obscenity, foolish talk or coarse joking, which are out of place, but rather thanksgiving.*
>
> *Eph 4:29 Do not let any unwholesome talk come out of your mouths, but only what is helpful for building others up*

according to their needs, that it may benefit those who listen

Eph 5:12   For it is shameful even to mention what the disobedient do in secret.

Col 3:8   But now you must rid yourselves of all such things as these: anger, rage, malice, slander, and filthy language from your lips.

It is important that we teach our children to be pure in thought, speech, and action. They must learn from us to avoid all vulgarity that would consist of profanity, dirty jokes, toilet humor, and obscene gestures.

10

Expectations for Different Children and Different Ages

"Sometimes, a child is not as handicapped by his condition as parents are by their low expectations."

One of the biggest obstacles in successful parenting is ignorance of the capabilities of a child at each stage of development. Typically, first-time parents are most aware of their ignorance and ask questions like, "How old will she be before she can sleep through the night?" or "When can I expect my little one to obey me?" Sadly, the ones often giving them advice are old-time parents who themselves lack proper understanding about children's capabilities. Unaware that children need not go through modern phases like the "terrible twos" and the "trying threes," they infect first-time parents with the misconceptions they developed from their own experiences with improper training. And the cycle continues.

When looking at various cultures throughout the world one realizes that God has equipped children with far more capabilities than most American parents understand. In many socially undeveloped countries children can work capably and diligently at home by 5 years of age. In those same "backward" countries young men might be starting their careers by age 12.

One need only look back in American history to discover the same thing.

In 1778 John Quincy Adams served in an ambassadorial post in the court of Catherine the Great in Russia – he was 14 years old. In 1813, U.S. naval officer, David Farragut, commanded a captured British vessel – he was 12 years old, having begun his naval career at 9. These men were not unique in their culture. They were typical of the young adult teens of their day. Needless to say, preschool age children were beyond our modern youngsters in areas of personal responsibility. What we must learn from this is that unruly two year olds and rebellious teenagers are creations of our modern approach to child rearing.

Does the thought of an 18-month-old sitting peacefully during Sunday morning worship service appeal to you? Can you imagine a den in which the stereo does not have to be moved out of reach from a toddler because he has been trained to not touch? Are you able to envision a home where the Christmas tree is not kept safe in a playpen and where 8 year olds do their own laundry? Children are far more capable than most parents realize.

In order to bring our children into their greatest potential we must lose our fear of "warping their little psyche" by requiring submission of their will to ours. We must not be afraid of "robbing them of their childhood" when we emphasize responsibility before play. Let us be careful of selling our children short when we say things like, "Kids will be kids," or "They're only children." Yes, they are not as capable as adults, but they are far more capable than we give them credit.

WHAT CAN BE EXPECTED AT WHAT AGE?

Susanna Wesley wrote as one of her rules in her "Plan of Education":

> *"When turned a year old (and some before), they were taught to fear the rod and to cry softly, by which means they escaped abundance of correction which they might otherwise have had . . ."*[1]

Mrs. Wesley had found, that children were capable of understanding correction by 1 year of age. Her conviction was not unique. Parents throughout history have held a similar philosophy. How far we have fallen!

The premise for training children is the same no matter what their age: *If they can understand you, they can be trained to obey you.*

HOW CAN PARENTS TELL IF THEIR CHILD UNDERSTANDS?

Consider the following exercises:

- *Tone* and *manner:* By 9 months old, children may not understand all your words, but most can read your *tone* and *manner.* They understand a firm "No," perfectly – that is why they cry in response.

- *Restraint:* The crawler who struggles to get down from your arms should not be rewarded. Be sure to say "No" and hold him tight until he stops struggling, and then do not put him down for a while. He is

---

[1] Cited by Rebecca Lamar Harmon, *Susanna, Mother of the Wesleys* [Nashville, Tenn.: Abingdon, 1968] pp. 58-59

smart enough to learn that when Mommy or Daddy initiates an action he is to submit to it.

- *Offering a treat:* To test a toddler's understanding of your vocabulary, without showing him anything, offer him a familiar treat, like ice cream or a bottle. Does he respond? If he does, then he is old enough to understand a simple direction such as, "Come here, son," and should be chastised each time that he chooses to defy your authority.

- *The clap:* If your crawler reaches for the stereo, walk over, offer a firm "No" and clap your hands once. If they respond to your voice and the sharp sound of the clap and turn away, they got the message and should be held accountable from then on. You may even want to skip the clap.

BUT MY CHILD IS DIFFERENT!

Yes, your child is different. All children are different from one another, just like they will be when they are adults. One is proficient at math and another is better at spelling. People are born with different personalities and therefore, different capabilities. Some are more proficient in the areas of art, athletics, humor, intelligence, and social awareness. Some can sit for hours and read, while others always lose at Freeze Tag, not realizing that their "frozen" body is in constant motion.

Some children learn and progress at faster paces than others. Some cannot seem to remember anything and others remember too much. Yes, children are all different, but God's standards are the same.

CAN DIFFERENT CHILDREN BE HELD TO THE SAME STANDARD?

It is true – every child is different from all others, but that does not mean they can be held to different standards. God's standards are the same for everyone. Kindness is kindness, respect is respect, obedience is obedience, and rudeness is rudeness. God's standards do not change from child to child – they may be harder to achieve with one child than another, but like God, His standards are eternal and unchangeable.

DANGERS OF THE STATEMENT "MY CHILD IS DIFFERENT"

The statement, "My child is different," is a dangerous statement. In one context, a parent may say it simply referring to the personality differences between children, but all too often it is an attempt to justify a child's disobedience. Sadly, the parent who believes that his child's rudeness, spite, or selfishness, is just a personality bent, ultimately handicaps himself in his parenting. Parents must know their children are capable or they will not hold them to God's standard.

Often, the parent who believes his child is just "different" is really saying, *"I've tried my best and I don't know what else to do."* The good news is that there is hope. Your child may simply have become a victim of your blind spots. It could very well be that this book will be the avenue of transformation in your home.

WHAT ABOUT SPECIAL NEEDS CHILDREN?

Special needs kids are just that – *special*. They may be handicapped by autism, retardation, or brain damage. Possibly they have been diagnosed with Attention Deficit Disorder,[2] or they may have been a drug baby who still suffers the side effects of their birth mother's heroin addiction. For their parents who know and love them, these children can be a source of joy, but as those same parents may testify, they can also be a source of great grief. For with the delight of parenting comes the pain of watching your child struggle with anti-social behavior, which brings them rejection from others and trouble at home.

Some parents of special needs children find consolation in knowing that their child's misbehavior is rooted in a chemical imbalance or a brain dysfunction, but that comfort may vacillate, depending how much stress they cause at home. Many of these parents, distressed by their child's misbehavior, are haunted by the nagging question, "Is there something else I can do?" There certainly is.

With such varying degrees of mental handicap facing different children, a common basis for determining trainability must be established. The parent of each child must determine, *"To what degree has my child shown himself to be trainable in the past?"*

Parents, determine: Can they . . .
- feed themselves?

---

[2] Although the validity of A.D.D. as a scientifically provable "disability" is understandably questioned by some, its predictable patterns of behavior, at the least, are indicative of inherited personality traits.

- dress themselves?
- visit the toilet by themselves?
- get a drink of water from the tap?
- operate a VCR?
- complain when they are unhappy?

If they can do these things, how did they learn – by direct training and by watching? If they have shown they are trainable, why stop there?

Yes, they may have a brain dysfunction or chemical imbalance, but that is no excuse for rebellious, disrespectful, or unruly behavior. When you walk together, do not pull them by the arm or drag them along – require them to walk obediently with you. At meal times, unless they lack motor coordination, do not permit them to eat like a pig. When they are greeted by family friends, do not permit them to scream or run away. In being introduced to someone new, require them to be polite and to speak respectfully.

Yes, they are harder to train than a "normal" child, but God's standards are the same. In fact, the parent must apply the same principle of child training to the special needs child as to any child:[3]

- *Work to subdue the will.*

---

[3] Even many levels of autistic behavior, if caught early enough, can be trained out of a child. Such a child is not easily brought out of his self-involved world, but many parents who have given themselves to the time-consuming training, testify to its effectiveness.

- *Bring it into complete subjection to yours as early in their life as possible.*

- *Don't compromise God's standards. (Just as shyness is no excuse for rudeness, A.D.D. is no excuse for a lack of self-control.)*

- *Whatever moral behavior you want, set that as your goal, and go for it.*

That goal will be more difficult and may take longer to achieve than with a normal child, but it absolutely must be done. The longer one waits, the stronger the will grows, making it more difficult to subdue as the years go by.

Parents, have hope!

Sometimes, a child is not as handicapped by his condition as parents are by their low expectations. The parents who expect little of their child inadvertently degrade him by accepting that soul-less animals are more trainable. Consider – since, contrary to their nature, wild animals can be domesticated and trained to perform difficult feats, *we can be sure that special needs children can be trained as well!* Few parents would admit they believed that their children were lower in ability than animals, but their low expectations of them infer it.

MY PERSONAL NOTE TO THE SPECIAL NEEDS PARENT

Of my six children, two have been clinically diagnosed with Attention Deficit Disorder, and one as A.D.H.D. (Hyperactive). Over the years, we have been the route of medications and support groups, but nothing has affected our children's behavior like the principles of biblically based child training. I have found dietary treatment for some conditions like A.D.D. and autism may be helpful, but balancing the body chemistry is no substitute for proper training. As parents of "special needs" children, we must be careful of allowing rebellious or disrespectful behavior, because we imagine it impossible to train our children to behave otherwise. Let us hold to God's standard and persevere in our training.

A key tip I offer any parent, but especially the parent of a particularly challenging child – be careful of allowing frustration to sour you towards that child. Listen to yourself – do you place an exclamation mark at the end of that one child's name in comparison to the others? Have you decided that his incessant moving of his body or tapping of his fingers is "rebellion"? Be careful! What we perceive as justified anger, will effectively communicate a lack of acceptance. Eventually, that child will not seek acceptance from you, but will find it from someone you will deem a dangerous influence. Be firm, but draw your child into obedience by your love and acceptance. Intimidation may conform the outside for a while, but you will lose his heart, and ultimately your ability to influence him. (More in chapter 15.)

——— 11 ———

Rehearsing Right Behavior

"The best defense is a good offense."
Atilla the Hun

TEACHING OBEDIENCE THROUGH REHEARSING PROPER BEHAVIOR

An important principle of successful repentance, although plainly displayed in the Bible, is often missed by many believers in their reading. Ephesians 4:28 reveals it clearly. There we read, *"He who has been stealing must steal no longer, but must work, doing something useful with his own hands, that he may have something to share with those in need."* We are told here, as we are throughout the epistles, that we are not simply to cease from *wrong* behavior, but instead are to do *right* behavior. Trying to stop sinful habits without replacing them with righteous ones will frustrate any adult Christian, let alone a child. Anyone who goes out each day and tries simply to "not sin" is bound for failure, ie: trying to "not be angry" at your boss all day will never get the success as "pursuing love" for your boss.

Our children, in order to learn how to obey us, must understand not only what they must *not* do, but what they are *to* do. This will require us to help them plan proper responses to life and temptations. Not only must we help them identify and plan a path of repentance, but we must also prepare them to walk it by rehearsing with them in advance of the situation.

140

- The parents who know their children tend to give in to their shyness when meeting new adults, can practice in advance of an upcoming encounter. They can role-play the situation and give them the opportunity to rehearse proper responses, ie: *"Hello, Mrs. Smith. Come in and have a seat. I'll tell my mother you're here."*

- In a store when your children start enjoying the displays as a playground, call them over to you and say, *"Please come stand by me and be bored."* (Remember the best response to the child complaining of boredom: *"I'm glad to hear you are bored. You will find as you grow that life is full of boring moments, so it is important for you to learn to endure boredom now."*)

- Rather than waiting until Sunday morning and using a church worship service to teach a child to sit still, it is helpful to have them practice at home – not as punishment, but as a training exercise to help them get their little bodies under control. Pull up a chair, and have them sit quietly for increasing increments of time. Try 5 minutes the first day, 10 the second, 15 the third, and so on. Chastise them each time they get down without permission. Start when they are toddlers and you will be amazed at what they are capable. This is a very simple means of teaching them first-time obedience.

- Plan their responses for them, giving them not only the bad behavior to avoid, but the good behavior to pursue:
    - WRONG: *"Johnny, when that boy pushes you, don't fight."*
    - RIGHT: *"Johnny, when that boy pushes you, come tell me."* Children need their paths clearly

laid out for them. Just as they need to know what NOT to do, they need to know what TO do.

- If you have picked them up and they do not want to be held, do not put them down when they fuss or try to wriggle from your arms. Teach them to ask politely, *"May I get down, please?"*

- A child who is learning to submit his will to his parents should be required to respond with a *verbal* affirmation to all instructions. It is an important exercise of coming under parental authority and increases the likelihood of obedience. Give them the acceptable responses and have them rehearse saying it, ie:
  - *"Yes, Mom"* or *"Yes, Dad,"*; *"I will obey you, Dad"*; *"I will stay in bed, Dad."*
  - Children can respond with anything you require of them, like my wife's favorite: *"Yes, Mother, most beautiful among women."*
  - Even toddlers, with limited speech, can learn to be polite, by hearing their parent suggest for them proper polite responses, ie: After a diaper change, you say for them, *"Thank you for changing my diaper, Dad,"* or after a meal you say, *"Thank you for making dinner, Mom."*

Pick the battlefield

Rather than waiting until you are pressed for time to train your children, consider setting times for training their wills. Don't wait for them to misbehave, forcing you to act only in response. Instead, plan and initiate time for their training.

For example, if you want your toddlers to learn to obey your word, set 10 minutes aside each day to train them to obey your voice. Pick a time in which you will have nothing better to do than train them. Then find them in the house and call them to come to you. Speak to them calmly, and only one time. If they do not come, walk over, pick them up, look them in the eye, and say, "When Mommy or Daddy speaks to you, you must obey," and then administer proper chastisement. Place them down on the floor where they were, walk away from them, and call them again. Repeat the process until they come each time. Walk to different places in the room, or walk out of the room and call them. After they consistently obey, keep practicing with them for a few more minutes. Be sure to praise and affirm them each time they obey, and you will discover that they find joy in pleasing you.

What this accomplishes:

- Typically, within minutes, your children will be capable of obeying you.
- Their wills become subdued and they begin the process of learning to say "No" to themselves.
- They become conditioned to respond to your voice.
- As they become conditioned to obey your voice, you will find that their obedience carries over to other areas of life, ie: they obey you more readily at bedtime, at mealtime, in public, etc.

You can practice with various other basic commands, such as, "Don't touch." "Put that down." "Stop." "Sit down." "Don't move, stay there." "Be quiet – close your lips." The more regularly you take time aside to train your children's wills, the sooner you will see them become ready to receive values instruction.

— 12 —

Children and Food

"Starving children in third world countries are rarely found to be picky eaters."

SHOULD CHILDREN BE REQUIRED TO EAT AND ACCEPT THANKFULLY FOODS THEY DO NOT ENJOY?

(Concerning a *pattern* of pickiness and not random occasions of appetite loss)

Reasons why parents are reluctant to require children to regularly eat foods they don't enjoy:

- They are concerned children may gag or vomit.

- They fear it will make children have a negative attitude toward food.

- They want to reduce stress at mealtime. It is easier to train their will all day in other areas of home life.

- They are empathetic. They do not enjoy certain foods, so do not want to force a child to eat something they do not like.

Reasons why parents should require children to eat food prepared for them:

- Requiring them to receive the food their parents have chosen for them teaches them to submit to parental authority. In doing so their will is subdued. If neglected their will is strengthened.

- Submission to parental decisions teaches trust in parental wisdom.

- Food is an area in which the will is most visible in a young child thereby providing the *optimum* opportunity to subdue it.

- It teaches them good manners. Ungratefulness is rude. It is impolite and insulting to refuse a gift, especially one that has been labored over. It is particularly disrespectful and thankless to refuse the food God has provided for the family. Food God provides should be received with thankfulness. (Mt 14:19; 15:36; 26:26; Lk 24:30; John 6:23; Acts 27:35; Rom 14:6; 1 Tim 4:3-4)

- Food is a gift for which we give thanks – first to God and then to the one who prepared it. We teach our children hypocrisy if we encourage them to thank God for the food He provided and then allow them to continually reject it. (Ps 145:15; Job 36:31)

- It will help prevent them from becoming picky eaters. Picky eating is generally considered a negative trait. As adults they will lose respect when they refuse to eat the food set before them while guests in others' homes. Children in the same situation can bring shame on their family.

- Picky eating is a trait found predominantly in a spoiled and affluent society. Starving children in third world countries are rarely found to be picky eaters. Parents pamper by permitting pickiness.

- If children are consistently allowed to refuse nutritious foods, they will become malnourished.

- Moms will lean towards preparing only foods that the children will eat, thereby granting the children authority to control the family menu.

- It is important to get children used to taking on difficult tasks. Requiring them to develop a taste for food they do not at first enjoy teaches them that by self-denial difficult things in life can be faced and overcome.

- Acquiring a taste for food is more easily learned when young. Waiting until adulthood to develop that discipline is far more difficult.

Each child is born with a self-centered worldview, so expects his wants to be satisfied. Requiring him to eat whatever is given him helps subdue his natural demand for gratification, and he learns that what he wants in life is not as important as what his parents want for him. This submission to parents is a key part in the subduing of the self-will and the development of maturity.

Exasperating Your Child

"Most parents are afraid of exasperating their children by being too firm, but most children are exasperated by parents who are not firm consistently."

25 SURE WAYS TO EXASPERATE YOUR CHILDREN

1. Never admit you are wrong. Always be right. Acknowledge no mistakes – excuse, justify, and rationalize every error.

2. Model hypocrisy. Hold them to a higher standard than you hold for yourself. Require perfectly of them that which you fail in *miserably.*

3. Fail to keep promises. Frustrate them and teach them to mistrust your word by rarely following through on that which you say you will do for them.

4. Demand too much of them. Tolerate nothing less than perfection. Catch their every failure and stay on them when they fall short of your perfect standard. Know no mercy.

5. Over-protect them. No matter how old they are, limit their freedom and independence. Give them few opportunities to fail. Make all decisions for them, without consideration for their feelings or desires.

6. Batter them with words. Rather than responding to misbehavior with appropriate disciplinary actions, habitually lecture them for long periods of time.

7. Abuse them verbally. Bark out your orders. Yell at them when they blow it. Let your tone consistently demonstrate harshness. Demean them by name-calling, character assassination, and predictions of failure. Swear at them when they tick you off.

8. Make discipline too severe. Mete out punishments that are overly harsh for the crime.

9. Show favoritism towards their brothers or sisters. Give unequal disciplines for similar violations. Consistently trust one child over the other. During correction, compare them to their siblings. Respond harshly to one child and sweetly to another for the same infraction.

10. Embarrass them. Show them disrespect by scolding or disciplining them in front of others, particularly in front of their teenage friends. Talk openly about their weakness and mistakes to others.

11. Give no time warnings. When they are in the middle of a fun activity, never give advance warning that it is time to end it. Regularly wait until the last minute and demand them to immediately stop whatever they are doing. *(However, because life doesn't always give advance warnings, do not be afraid, when necessary, to teach them to respond to disappointments by requiring that they end their activities abruptly, and with a good attitude.)*

12. Try to be their buddy. Strive to be their parent and their pal. Tease, chat, and play with them like a peer one moment and step into your superior role to exercise adult authority the next. Permit them to show disrespect to you, teasing you, correcting you, playfully calling you names, and then turn around and exercise firm authority over them in some matter. Allowing them such over-familiarity will frustrate them, because they will be made to feel like equals *and* subordinates. The insecure parent who needs his children's approval will find his children despising him. Children innately need their parents to be *leaders* not *followers*.

13. Withhold firm discipline and proper training. The lack of clear boundaries will make them insecure in your love. The responsibility they will bear in over-seeing and making decisions for your family will produce in them anxiety too great for their emotional maturity.

14. Discipline inconsistently. Most parents are afraid of exasperating their children by being too firm, but most children are frustrated by parents who are not firm consistently. Enforcing rules inconsistently sets unclear boundaries, which beg to be violated. It is also like giving them occasional permission to disobey. The temptation to risk violating your standards leaves them insecure and anxious. If you make a rule – enforce it. Otherwise, your kids will "stress out" trying to figure when to take you seriously.

15. Assert parental authority weakly. Not only will you exasperate your kids with inconsistent discipline, but you will also frustrate them by sending mixed messages. With your lips you will say, "NO, and that's final," but you will permit them to bring up the subject over and over, and you may eventually cave in. Your words draw a line, but you allow them to step over it. The parents whose limits are not firm, allow their children to partially shoulder responsibility for running the home – a job for which they have not been equipped. They are always planning, plotting, and scheming. There is no rest for the child who is always testing their parents to see how far they can be pushed.

16. Consistently believe evil of them.
In correcting misdeeds, jump on them like you expected the worst, as if you are picking up where you left off last time. Communicate to them your mistrust by rarely greeting them with a smile. Let them see you looking at them suspiciously whenever they come into your presence. In correction, remind them of all the times they have failed throughout their lifetime. Give them no genuine fresh starts.

17. Do not listen to them. Give them no opportunity for expression of their opinions, complaints, or frustrations. Refuse to allow them to speak their mind, even when communicated respectfully.

18. Continually criticize and critique them when they share their innermost feelings and thoughts. When they are being vulnerable, expose their hidden heart motives. Tease them about sensitive issues.

19. Communicate to them how unwanted they are. Let them know they are an inconvenient nuisance, that you could have had a successful career if it was not for them. Allow them to overhear you promise others that you will not have any more children, and that you will be glad when they move out of the house. Let them hear you speak to others about "children" with regret or contempt in your voice. When you are angry at them, tell them you hate them.

20. Threaten them with rejection. When they misbehave, frequently warn them that they may have to leave home. If they are a child of divorce, hold over their heads that they may have to go live with their other parent.

21. Never communicate to them approval. Force them to hunt for it outside the home from their friends, teachers, or youth leaders. Find fault with everything they do. Never allow them to think they have satisfied you.

22. Neglect them. Always be too busy to give them *positive* time. Give them attention only when they need discipline.

23. Overindulge them. Allow them such an influential voice in family decisions that they will come to expect that they should have their way. They will think of the family as a democracy, and therefore will resent any parental decisions made without their input. Permit them so many personal decisions when young, that by their teen years, they will think they have a right to run their own life. Grant them so many of their wishes, that they will think they are owed everything, and will appreciate nothing.

24. Reward insolence. When they express themselves angrily or speak to you with disrespect, reward them by allowing continued discussion. When they do not get their way, and they sulk or pout, don't discipline them, try hard to cheer them up. Distract them. Buy them a treat. Cave in and change your mind. You will send them the message that they are in charge and you fear their disapproval. As the years go on they will become more and more angry when they do not get their way. After all, you have accidentally sent them the message that they should have it.

25. Cease a time of chastisement before it has produced humility. This is probably the greatest cause of exasperated children. Parents attempt to subdue the will through biblical chastisement, but they end each attempt before the child has humbled himself and accepted responsibility for his actions. Many parents fight strong-willed, angry adolescents, because they consistently failed to bring humility through discipline. Each time of chastisement only evokes more and more anger. (See chapter 5, "How to Tell When a Time of Discipline is Completed")

——— 14 ———

Sheltering Children

"Kids have to face real life some time – you can't protect them forever."

Line often spoken by parents who do not understand their God-given responsibility to oversee and direct their children.

Most parents love their children. They want what is best for them and would give their lives to protect them. However, despite their protective concern, too few parents stop to consider the spiritual and moral dangers of the day-to-day situations in which they place their children. They have wrongly considered to be *absolutes* things like school, youth group, choir, summer camp, sports, friends, theater productions, music, dances, dating, Sunday school, Christian clubs, etc. None of these are inherently evil, but each puts your children under the authority or influence of someone else – someone who does not love your children as much as you do, nor will be held accountable on Judgment Day for them.

Accepting variables as absolutes

Is it possible that one or all of those activities or settings has more of a corrupting than a redeeming influence on your children? Could it be that a member of the youth group will introduce your son to drugs, or seduce your daughter at summer camp? Is it possible that your son's rebellious attitude might disappear if you removed him from his school or prohibited him being with certain friends?

These hypothetical possibilities are not offered because this book's agenda is to get you to pull your children out of these activities. They are offered to help you reevaluate those things you have considered to be absolutes. Some of these activities might be completely safe and have no negative impact on the goals of your child training, but then again, they might *all* be dangerous. Too many parents have thwarted their own efforts at training up godly children, because they assumed they needed to send them off to a community program or to a church-sponsored event.

Let us not repeat Israel's parenting mistakes. They were given guidelines for raising their children[1] and were admonished to keep them from intimate association with the pagan inhabitants of the Promised Land.[2] God knew the pagan influence would be so infectious that He commanded Israel to drive out every non-Israelite. Read His warnings in Deut 8:19-20; Ex 23:32-33; 34:12; Num 33:51-56; and Josh 23:7,12-13. The book of Judges reveals how every new generation of Israelites grew up, and were drawn into idolatry and rebellion against God, because their parents disregarded God's prohibitions and warnings.[3] Learning from Israel's mistakes may save you years of

---

[1] Deut 6:6-9; 11:16-23
[2] Deut 7:1-6, 16
[3] Judges 1:27-33; 2:3

heartache. (Also read Proverbs 13:20; 23:17; 24:1; 1 Cor 15:33.)

Parents, consider – none of our traditional American childhood experiences absolutely has to happen. They are *variables* in life. The only absolute is that we must raise up offspring who love God and emulate his character. We must chase from our minds the idea that children will only be fulfilled in childhood if they have certain traditional experiences. We must erase the thought that children can only be prepared for "real life" by being immersed in worldly influences and experiencing overwhelming temptation. Israelite children were vulnerable and their parents failed to protect them. We must not repeat Israel's mistakes.

As conscientious parents we must ask ourselves, what good will it do our children to spend multiple hours each week under the influence of those who may corrupt their values or tempt them to sin? Childhood is so brief, why would we want them to spend excessive amounts of time doing something that offers no spiritual value, and does little to bring them to maturity?

If maturity is developed by denying self and responsibly serving others, and immaturity is fed by spending excessive time in self-indulging, entertainment oriented activities, why would we want our children to spend multiple hours each week involved in such things? We must evaluate their pursuits and decide if the time and energy required will actually make them mature and prepare them for their adult roles.

What variables have you made into absolutes? Mom, do you really need that job, or do your children need you more? Dad, has greater income become more important than time with your kids? Are you justifying keeping them in that particular school, because it is convenient, despite its obvious corrupting influence? If you fear for your son's well-being, because his soccer teammates seem to be having a greater negative influence on him than he is having a positive one on them, who says you have to leave him on the team? Have you accepted as an absolute that teenagers have to have bad attitudes? How big of a sacrifice are you willing to make to properly care for your children?

Parents, receive this challenge to reevaluate your absolutes and do only what is best for your children.

─── 15 ───
BEYOND OBEDIENCE:
Raising Children who Love God and Others

"Do nothing out of selfish ambition or vain conceit, but in humility consider others better than yourselves. Each of you should look not only to your own interests, but also to the interests of others. 5 Your attitude should be the same as that of Christ Jesus"
Philippians 2:3-5

THE GOOD THING:

As we established in chapter 2, children must learn to honor and obey their parents. As they do they develop the virtue of self-control that lays the foundation for maturity, and prepares their hearts to receive moral instruction from their parents.

THE TROUBLING THING:

Many parents grasp the importance of raising obedient, respectful children, but fail to understand the significance of raising them to be lovers of God and others. They assume that a self-governing child, raised in the Christian faith, will automatically grow to spiritual maturity as they grow in physical and mental maturity. However, such parents often discover that when their children reach adulthood, they may not continue in the morality or faith that their parents sought to give them. Even more frightening, some parents *are* content with the results of their parenting, but shouldn't be. They are satisfied that their children have grown up and remain active in the church, but these grownup children lack the most important Christian virtue – *love*.

As followers of Christ we must raise children who not only have the virtue of self-control, but who are lovers of God and true lovers of their families,[1] neighbors,[2] and enemies.[3]

Sadly, many parents do not value love as the highest virtue in their own personal lives, and therefore content themselves with simply raising their children to be obedient. They justify such an approach, insisting Christ taught that those who learn to obey are learning to love. Obedience certainly can be a trait of love,[4] but to subdue our children's wills and then neglect to teach them to love is like building the foundation for a house, and then stopping construction. The foundation is absolutely necessary, but the goal is the house. So too, obedience and respect which spring from a subdued self-will represent important elements of the foundation, but they are just that – foundational elements for the building of love.

---

[1] Love is proven not by how we treat the needy, but by how we treat our families. (1 Tim 5:8)

[2] Luke 10:29-37

[3] Love is proven not by how we treat our friends, but how we treat those who oppose us. (Mat 5:46-47)

[4] *John 14:15 "If you love me, you will obey what I command."*

Parents, gauge your values. Will you be satisfied if your children are obedient and respectful, serve in church ministries, wear conservative clothes, have neatly groomed hair, and listen only to hymns? These things may be good signs, but not if the children are socially cold and grow up with no concern for the lost or noticeable love for others, not if they are so self-involved that they avoid meeting new people and are not accustomed to reaching out to strangers, or opening their homes to the needy.

Check your goals. Will you be satisfied if your children can quote the entire Westminster Shorter Catechism, are so self-governing that they are able to sit silent and motionless in church for hours at a time, and are so well-behaved that wherever you walk they remain right by your side? Such self-restrained actions are a good foundation, but may be meaningless if they continually gossip, criticize, and demean others.

Will you be content if your sons wear suits to church and your daughters modest dresses, if they are known to be hardworking and responsible, and they address all adults as Mr. and Mrs.? If so, do not overlook their heart condition that allows them to continually bicker at home, and be unkind to all who offend them.

What if your children are as well mannered at home as they are in public, and their only flaw is their tendency to point out the shortcomings of others? We are foolish to be happy if our children's only imperfection is their arrogance, for God resists the proud.[5] A well-behaved proud child is useless to his

---

[5] James 4:6

fellow man and just as displeasing to God as a defiant rebel.[6]

THE REAL THING:

We know from Christ's teaching that the highest priority for his followers is that they love God preeminently, and be as devoted to their neighbors as they are to themselves.[7] Therefore, as we rear our children our chief goal must be to raise them to love God and their neighbors.

The apostle Paul reinforced this when he declared to his spiritual children that the goal of his instruction was not simply that they have right knowledge, but that whatever they learned from him would cause them to love.[8] Quite naturally, then, love was the quality he

---

[6] *Luke 18:10 "Two men went up to the temple to pray, one a Pharisee and the other a tax collector. 11 The Pharisee stood up and prayed about himself: 'God, I thank you that I am not like other men--robbers, evildoers, adulterers--or even like this tax collector. 12 I fast twice a week and give a tenth of all I get.' 13 "But the tax collector stood at a distance. He would not even look up to heaven, but beat his breast and said, 'God, have mercy on me, a sinner.' 14 "I tell you that this man, rather than the other, went home justified before God. For everyone who exalts himself will be humbled, and he who humbles himself will be exalted."* See also Mat 21:31; Mark 2:17; John 9:39-41; 1 Tim 3:6

[7] *Mat 22:37 Jesus replied: "'Love the Lord your God with all your heart and with all your soul and with all your mind.' 38 This is the first and greatest commandment. 39 And the second is like it: 'Love your neighbor as yourself.'*

[8] *1 Tim 1:5 But the goal of our instruction is love from a pure heart and a good conscience and a sincere faith.*

affirmed most often in letters to the churches.[9] Even when he told the Thessalonian church that they loved so well that they didn't need further teaching about it, he still proceeded to instruct them to love more and more.[10] And in Paul's first letter to the church at Corinth God made it quite clear that no matter what we accomplish or how spiritual we get, if we fail to love, it is worthless.[11]

So, if we raise children who have the ability to speak in the tongues of angels, have the faith to move mountains, perform deeds of self-sacrificing benevolence, and can obey in a flash with total respect, but lack love, we have accomplished *nothing*. Zip. Zero. Nada. Yes, obedient, self-governing children are beautiful and necessary, but if they do not *love* they lack the quality most dear to the heart of our God.

THE GREATEST THING:

Based on the supreme commandment, we know that the greatest thing in parenting is to raise children

---

[9] Eph 1:15; Phil 1:9; Col 1:4-5, 8; 1 Thes 1:3; 3:6, 12; 4:9-10; 2 Thes 1:3; Phile 1:5, 7

[10] *1 Th 4:9-10 Now about brotherly love we do not need to write to you, for you yourselves have been taught by God to love each other. 10 And in fact, you do love all the brothers throughout Macedonia. Yet we urge you, brothers, to do so more and more.*

[11] *1 Corinthians 13:1-3 "Though I speak with the tongues of men and of angels, but have not love, I have become sounding brass or a clanging cymbal. 2 And though I have the gift of prophecy, and understand all mysteries and all knowledge, and though I have all faith, so that I could remove mountains, but have not love, I am nothing. 3 And though I bestow all my goods to feed the poor, and though I give my body to be burned, but have not love, it profits me nothing."*

to love God. The apostle John teaches us that those who love God, do so because they first experience His love.[12] We must make it our goal therefore, to somehow convey God's love to our kids. The following four steps should aid any parent in helping their children to grow in love with God.

1. **Teach them the doctrinal truth of the gospel: God loves sinners**

But God demonstrates his own love for us in this: While we were still sinners, Christ died for us. 9 Since we have now been justified by his blood, how much more shall we be saved from God's wrath through him! 10 For if, when we were God's enemies, we were reconciled to him through the death of his Son, how much more, having been reconciled, shall we be saved through his life! Romans 5:8

Therefore, I tell you, her many sins have been forgiven--for she loved much. But he who has been forgiven little loves little." Luke 7:47

For us to pass on to our children the Truth that will cause them to grow in love with God, we must first understand it ourselves. When God sent His son as an atoning sacrifice for our sins, it wasn't because we deserved His love. Quite the opposite, we deserved His wrath. God is a righteous and holy judge who saw us not as good, lovable beings deserving of His love and mercy, but as sinners who offended Him. That is what makes Him so wonderful – He loves those who deserve to be *judged*. The gospel is glorious, because it is about

---

[12] *1 John 4:19 We love him, because he first loved us*

God having mercy on His enemies, personally paying off a debt His enemies owed to Him.

When we first call upon Christ we do so because we know we are "sinners" in need of a savior. However, many saved sinners fail to comprehend the depth of mercy they needed from God. They do not see the severity of their sinfulness, so do not appreciate the greatness of God's mercy. As Jesus taught – those who grasp the depth of their sinfulness, will love God all the more.[13]

To love God with all our hearts we must see that we did not merit the forgiveness Christ's death provided – we deserved the death itself. God hated our wickedness, but poured out His wrath on His innocent son instead of us.

In depicting our sinful condition, God describes our hearts as desperately wicked and deceitful above all things.[14] Until we receive from Him a new nature in salvation,[15] every motive we have is polluted and corrupt.[16] Our best deeds, He says, are like filthy rags.[17] In fact, God is so holy and pure that next to Him the sun is not bright,[18] and we are like maggots and worms.[19] God sees us as totally depraved sinners,[20]

---

[13] Luke 7:47

[14] Jer 17:9; Job 15:15-16; 25:4-6; Mark 7:20-23; John 2:24-5; Rom 3:10-18

[15] 2 Cor 5:17

[16] Gen.6:5; 8:21;

[17] Isa 64:6

[18] Job 15:15-16; 25:4-6

[19] Job 25:5-6

[20] Ps 14:2-3; 51:5; Eccl 7:29

and when Christ sacrificed himself on the cross he suffered the wrath God felt toward us in our sins.

What love this is! The perfect and pure, God of the universe suffered a horrible death for those He counted as enemies. We offend the Righteous Judge and instead of executing sentence upon us, condemning us to eternal punishment, He suffers our death sentence for us. He reaches out and loves the very sinners who deserve His wrath. What a merciful God!

Parents, we must grasp this Truth for ourselves, and pass it on to our children. If they are to fall in love with God they must understand the depth of the gospel.

2. **Teach them who God is – the most amazing and lovable being who has ever existed**

> *... And I pray that you, being rooted and established in love, 18 may have power, together with all the saints, to grasp how wide and long and high and deep is the love of Christ, 19 and to know this love that surpasses knowledge--that you may be filled to the measure of all the fullness of God. Ephesians 3:17-19*

When we truly understand the gospel message we come to know God as incredibly lovable. Yet, even aside from seeing the mercy revealed on the cross, those who know Him find themselves in awe of Him and enamored with Him. The old expression "to know Him is to love Him" must have started with God. If we want our children to love God, then in the words of author, Tedd Tripp, "Dazzle them with God!"[21]

---

[21] From the seminar, Shepherding a Child's Heart

Do you know anyone who is "dazzled" with God? Do you know what that looks like, and do you know what it is about God that dazzles them? One who was enthralled with God was King David – he was thoroughly smitten with Him. So fulfilled was he by his intimate relationship with his Heavenly Father he once declared *"... As the deer pants for streams of water, so my soul pants for you, O God. 2 My soul thirsts for God, for the living God. When can I go and meet with God?"*[22] And again, *"One thing I ask of the LORD, this is what I seek: that I may dwell in the house of the LORD all the days of my life, to gaze upon the beauty of the LORD and to seek him in his temple."*[23]

The longer David got to know God the more he found Him to be absolutely and totally wonderful.

I have seen you in the sanctuary and beheld your power and your glory. 3 Because your love is better than life, my lips will glorify you. 4 I will praise you as long as I live, and in your name I will lift up my hands. 5 My soul will be satisfied as with the richest of foods; with singing lips my mouth will praise you. 6 On my bed I remember you; I think of you through the watches of the night. 7 Because you are my help, I sing in the shadow of your wings. 8 My soul clings to you; your right hand upholds me. Psalm 63:2-8

David loved God because he appreciated how He rescued and provided him safety in times of trouble.

But I will sing of your strength, in the morning I will sing of your love; for you are my fortress, my refuge in times of trouble. Psalm 59:16

---

[22] Ps 42:1-2
[23] Ps 27:4

From the ends of the earth I call to you, I call as my heart grows faint; lead me to the rock that is higher than I. 3 For you have been my refuge, a strong tower against the foe. 4 I long to dwell in your tent forever and take refuge in the shelter of your wings. Psalm 61:2

My soul finds rest in God alone; my salvation comes from him. 2 He alone is my rock and my salvation; he is my fortress, I will never be shaken. Psalm 62:1

David loved God for the wisdom and practical value of His laws.

Oh, how I love your law! I meditate on it all day long. Psalm 119:97

Your statutes are wonderful; therefore I obey them. Psalm 119:129

I obey your statutes, for I love them greatly. 168 I obey your precepts and your statutes, for all my ways are known to you. Psalm 119:167-168

The law of the LORD is perfect, reviving the soul. The statutes of the LORD are trustworthy, making wise the simple. Psalm 19:7

He found Him faithful and dependable.

For the word of the LORD is right and true; he is faithful in all he does. Psalm 33:4

Your kingdom is an everlasting kingdom, and your dominion endures through all generations. The LORD is faithful to all his promises and loving toward all he has made. Psalm 145:13

David was enthralled with God as the Creator.

Come, let us sing for joy to the LORD; let us shout aloud to the Rock of our salvation. 2 Let us come before him with thanksgiving and extol him with music and song. 3 For the LORD is the great God, the great King above all gods. 4 In his hand are the depths of the earth, and the mountain peaks belong to him. 5 The sea is his, for he made it, and his hands formed the dry land. 6 Come, let us bow down in worship, let us kneel before the LORD our Maker; 7 for he is our God and we are the people of his pasture, the flock under his care. Psalm 95:1-7

For you created my inmost being; you knit me together in my mother's womb. 14 I praise you because I am fearfully and wonderfully made; your works are wonderful, I know that full well. Psalm 139:13

He was in awe of God's omnipresence.

Where can I go from your Spirit? Where can I flee from your presence? 8 If I go up to the heavens, you are there; if I make my bed in the depths, you are there. Psalm 139:7-8

David was amazed by God's omniscience.

O LORD, you have searched me and you know me. 2 You know when I sit and when I rise; you perceive my thoughts from afar. 3 You discern my going out and my lying down; you are familiar with all my ways. 4 Before a word is on my tongue you know it completely, O LORD. 5 You hem me in--behind and before; you have laid your hand upon me. 6 Such knowledge is too wonderful for me, too lofty for me to attain. Psalm 139:1-6

He revered God for His incredible power.

The mountains melt like wax before the LORD, before the Lord of all the earth. Psalm 97:5

"How awesome are your deeds! So great is your power that your enemies cringe before you. Psalm 66:3

I have seen you in the sanctuary and beheld your power and your glory. 3 Because your love is better than life, my lips will glorify you. Psalm 63:2-3

Great is the LORD and most worthy of praise; his greatness no one can fathom. 4 One generation will commend your works to another; they will tell of your mighty acts. 5 They will speak of the glorious splendor of your majesty, and I will meditate on your wonderful works. 6 They will tell of the power of your awesome works, and I will proclaim your great deeds. Psalm 145:3-6

David feared God for His great authority

My flesh trembles in fear of you; I stand in awe of your laws. Psalm 119:120

You alone are to be feared. Who can stand before you when you are angry? Psalm 76:7

Who knows the power of your anger? For your wrath is as great as the fear that is due you. Psalm 90:11

If you, O LORD, kept a record of sins, O Lord, who could stand? 4 But with you there is forgiveness; therefore you are feared. Psalm 130:3-4

Taste and see that the LORD is good; blessed is the man who takes refuge in him. 9 Fear the LORD, you his saints, for those who fear him lack nothing ... 11 Come, my children, listen to me; I will teach you the fear of the LORD. Psalm 34:8-11

This chapter does not allow the space needed to help the reader discover all that is wonderful about our

Heavenly Father, but there is a path we can walk to meet Him. God makes a simple promise that He always fulfills. If we seek Him *with all our hearts* He will reveal Himself to us.[24] We must spend time in the Word with a hungry, humble heart, praying that there we will encounter God. If we are to help our children find God irresistible, we must know Him deeply ourselves.

3. **Model for them love for God**

> *I have set you an example that you should do as I have done for you. John 13:15*

> *... set an example for the believers in speech, in life, in love, in faith and in purity. 1 Tim 4:12b*

If you want your children to love God, then it will be important that you teach them to love Him by your example. The saying, "the most important things in life are *caught* not *taught*," is particularly true with our children. What we *do* teaches them more than what we *say*. Our words, in fact, may be of little influence if they are not matched by a genuine heart of love for God.

For the glory of God and for the sake of our children we must make it our goal to love the Lord with all our heart, mind, soul, and strength. Employing the best biblical parenting principles is good, but proper

---

[24] *Jer 29:13 'And you will seek Me and find Me, when you search for Me with all your heart. 14 'And I will be found by you,' declares the LORD ...*

discipline may not impact our children's souls if we fail to model a sincere love for God. We need to do both.[25]

A problem faced by some parents is that the "love for God" they model doesn't look to their children like love at all. Their children perceive the Christian life to be a loveless, joyless, preoccupation with avoiding bad stuff. Certainly, a critical aspect of walking with Christ is throwing off everything that hinders and the sin that entangles,[26] as well as avoiding harmful influences.[27] However, if it appears to our children that our Christian life is a drudgery and a burden, and our dominant concern is with what we must *avoid* and what we *don't do,* we must ask ourselves – will they want that? *We* don't even really want that for ourselves!

Parents – are your children drawn to your Jesus or is your "religion" just a burden they feel heaped upon them? Remember, Jesus cautioned the Jewish leaders against loading people down with burdens they could not carry.[28]

The Christian life is not simply about not doing bad stuff. It is not even about doing good in order to gain God's approval. A walk with Christ is a life of joyful thankfulness. It is daily enjoying God's love and mercy,

---

[25] King David is an example of one who modeled great passion for God, but whose children went astray, because he neglected to properly control them (1 Kings1:5-6). Eli and Samuel, both godly priests of Israel, also lost their children because they failed in the same way (1 Sam 3:13-14; 8:3).

[26] Heb 12:1

[27] 2 Cor 6:17 - 7:1; James 1:27

[28] Luke 11:46

and doing good for Him because He accepts us – not because we are striving to get accepted.[29]

When Jesus called followers to him, he said, *"Come to me, all you who are weary and burdened, and I will give you rest. 29 Take my yoke upon you and learn from me, for I am gentle and humble in heart, and you will find rest for your souls. 30 For my yoke is easy and my burden is light."*[30] The life Jesus has for his people is one of beauty. If our walks with him are a burden, and our souls have no rest, we are obviously missing what it means to live a life of love for God.

For our sake and for the sake of our children, may we all pursue what it means to be loved by God and love Him in return.

4. **Convey to them the love of God by loving them**

Dear friends, let us love one another, for love comes from God. Everyone who loves has been born of God and knows God. 8 Whoever does not love does not know God, because God is love ... 16 And so we know and rely on the love God has for us. God is love. Whoever lives in love lives in God, and God in him. 1 John 4:7-8, 16

Philip, the disciple, once requested of Jesus, *"Lord, show us the Father..."* To which he received the reply,

---

[29] *Rom 5:10 For if, when we were God's enemies, we were reconciled to him through the death of his Son, how much more, having been reconciled, shall we be saved through his life!*
Rom 2:4 Or do you show contempt for the riches of his kindness, tolerance and patience, not realizing that God's kindness leads you toward repentance?
[30] Mat 11:28

"Don't you know me, Philip, even after I have been among you such a long time? Anyone who has seen me has seen the Father. How can you say, 'Show us the Father'[31] Jesus' statement was not simply an affirmation of his deity, but was an illustration of how one person can be a reflection of another. So too, as children of God we can reflect Him and his love to our own children.

Have you ever stopped to consider that it was love that made Jesus attractive to sinners and allowed him to influence them? He spoke against sin, but he still drew sinners to himself. He hated evil, and preached for holiness, but those sinners who heard him, somehow knew he accepted them. In fact, so great and evident was his merciful love that he became known as the "friend of sinners."[32]

Zacchaeus, the despised tax collector, was a classic example of a sinner who was transformed by the love and acceptance of Christ. There he was up that tree, trying to get a good look at Jesus, when suddenly Jesus caught a glimpse of him. Christ responded by declaring, *"Zacchaeus, come down immediately. I must stay at your house today."* That was all it took. Zacchaeus' heart was changed. He instantly made a commitment to share his wealth with the needy and repay anyone from whom he had stolen.[33] *Christ's love caused him to love.*

Have you ever noticed that you are drawn to people who accept you, and you tend to avoid people who

---

[31] John 14:8-9
[32] Mat 11:19; 9:10-11; Luke 7:34; 15:1-2
[33] Luke 19:1-10

don't? And have you noticed that you listen more to people who have affection for you, and tend to resist those who are angry with you? Has it occurred to you that your children may be just like you?

Do you want your children to love your Jesus? Then it will be important that you love them with the same love God has for you. You will be attractive and they will want to know your Jesus. For the sake of our children, let us strive to understand all that love is.

THE SECOND GREATEST THING:

Christ taught that next to loving God, loving *others* should be the Christian's greatest pursuit.[34] Parents therefore, must teach their children from infancy that they are to love others as themselves. Those who make this a foundational goal of their child training will set their children dead center on the path to maturity and will establish in them the basis for respect of others.

If we want to teach our children to be as devoted to their siblings, neighbors, and enemies as they are to themselves, there are several steps we can take.

1. **Be certain you are first filled full with the love of Christ.**

Just like a dry well has no refreshment to offer, we will be unable to love others if we have not first drunk from God's spring. He is the source of all our compassion. He is the power behind our selfless care. Daily we must go to God to refresh ourselves in His love for us, and this love we must give to others.

---

[34] Mat 22:36-39; Phil 2:5-8

2. **Study the Scriptures to understand love in all of its facets.**

Our Lord was the picture of love. To grow in our knowledge of love we must study all that he taught and all that he did. The Greek word used to describe his love is agape, which conveys quite a depth of meaning:

• Love is a commitment based on a decision of the will, and not on emotion. It is not earned or deserved, but is unconditional. This means that we are never free to withhold love based on what another does. It is for this reason that Christ calls us to be gracious and merciful toward those who offend us, including users, abusers, and false accusers.

"But I tell you who hear me: Love your enemies, do good to those who hate you, 28 bless those who curse you, pray for those who mistreat you. 29 If someone strikes you on one cheek, turn to him the other also. If someone takes your cloak, do not stop him from taking your tunic. 30 Give to everyone who asks you, and if anyone takes what belongs to you, do not demand it back. Luke 6:27-30

Do not repay anyone evil for evil. Be careful to do what is right in the eyes of everybody. 18 If it is possible, as far as it depends on you, live at peace with everyone. 19 Do not take revenge, my friends, but leave room for God's wrath, for it is written: "It is mine to avenge; I will repay," says the Lord. 20 On the contrary: "If your enemy is hungry, feed him; if he is thirsty, give him something to drink. In doing this, you will heap burning coals on his head." 21 Do not be overcome by evil, but overcome evil with good. Rom 12:17-21

• Love is proven by sacrifice. We may have great affection for others, and even maintain a commitment to them, but if we are unwilling to inconvenience ourselves, we are missing a key ingredient of true love. Loving without cost may not be love at all. The sacrifices of love may be physical, emotional, or mental, and may include the yielding of personal rights.

> *Greater love has no one than this, that he lay down his life for his friends. John 15:13*[35]

> *This is how we know what love is: Jesus Christ laid down his life for us. And we ought to lay down our lives for our brothers. 1 John 3:16*

> *Your attitude should be the same as that of Christ Jesus: 6 Who, being in very nature God, did not consider equality with God something to be grasped, 7 but made himself nothing, taking the very nature of a servant, being made in human likeness. 8 And being found in appearance as a man, he humbled himself and became obedient to death-- even death on a cross! Phil 2:5-8*

• Love is not only sacrificial, but is *selfless* in its motives. It gives because the other needs, and not because it wants a return on the investment. It does not give to get. True love remains constant because it is given without strings and is not dependent on demands or expectations. The whole concept of loving another to get one's own needs met is entirely self-centered. Christ gave of himself not

---

[35] Also John 10:11; Rom 5:8

because he had need of us, but because we had need of him.

We who are strong ought to bear with the failings of the weak and not to please ourselves. 2 Each of us should please his neighbor for his good, to build him up. 3 For even Christ did not please himself... Rom 15:1-3

[Love] ... is not self-seeking, 1 Cor 13:5

But when you give a banquet, invite the poor, the crippled, the lame, the blind, 14 and you will be blessed. Although they cannot repay you, you will be repaid at the resurrection of the righteous." Luke 14:13

Nobody should seek his own good, but the good of others. 1 Cor 10:24

even as I try to please everybody in every way. For I am not seeking my own good but the good of many, so that they may be saved. 1 Cor 10:33

• Love cares for others so seeks to understand and relate with them. It is because we care that we are willing to forego what is comfortable to us, and put ourselves in another's place, either literally or empathetically.

For this reason he had to be made like his brothers in every way, in order that he might become a merciful and faithful high priest in service to God, and that he might make atonement for the sins of the people. 18 Because he himself suffered when he was tempted, he is able to help those who are being tempted. Heb 2:17-18

For we do not have a high priest who is unable to sympathize with our weaknesses, but we have one who has been tempted in every way, just as we are-- yet was without sin. Heb 4:15

Brothers, if someone is caught in a sin, you who are spiritual should restore him gently. But watch yourself, or you also may be tempted. 2 Carry each other's burdens, and in this way you will fulfill the law of Christ. Gal 6:1-2

• Love is empty if it is void of action. Warm words can be powerful, but just as faith is dead without works,[36] so also is love. Jesus taught that for love to be valid it must be expressed through our service of others.

Not so with you. Instead, whoever wants to become great among you must be your servant, 27 and whoever wants to be first must be your slave -- 28 just as the Son of Man did not come to be served, but to serve, and to give his life as a ransom for many." Mat 20:26-28[37]

Now that I, your Lord and Teacher, have washed your feet, you also should wash one another's feet. John 13:14

If anyone has material possessions and sees his brother in need but has no pity on him, how can the love of God be in him? 18 Dear children, let us not love with words or tongue but with actions and in truth. 1 John 3:17-18

---

[36] James 2:14-18
[37] Also Mat 23:11; Luke 22:25-27

• The love God has for us is outlined in the thirteenth chapter of 1 Corinthians. To understand His beautiful love will increase our appreciation of Him, as well as empower us to better love others and equip us to teach our children.

> *1 Cor 13:4 Love is patient, love is kind. It does not envy, it does not boast, it is not proud. 5 It is not rude, it is not self-seeking, it is not easily angered, it keeps no record of wrongs. 6 Love does not delight in evil but rejoices with the truth. 7 It always protects, always trusts, always hopes, always perseveres. 8 Love never fails ...*

WHAT ARE SOME PRACTICAL TIPS FOR RAISING LOVING CHILDREN?[38]

From the time they are born, we must elevate love as their life purpose.

1. Emphasize to them throughout their day that loving and serving others is our supreme goal. Evaluate all their social and moral decisions from the standpoint of love.

2. Make frequent opportunities for the family to serve others, ie: looking after widows or single moms, visiting convalescent hospitals, volunteering at the local Crisis Pregnancy Center, etc.

3. Encourage the children to surprise their siblings by secretly serving them, ie: doing their chores for them, making their beds, etc.

---

[38] Adapted from my seminar, "The Delightful Family"

4. Make the absence of love the issue of every childish dispute. When children are in conflict do not just rebuke them for fighting, but admonish them for *not loving*. Don't ask them "Who started it?" Ask them each how have they failed to love the other.

5. Frequently fill their hearts with your loving affection. Since a fresh dose of God's love fills the heart of a new believer with love for others,[39] consider that bickering children may respond powerfully to a moment of strong fatherly affection, ie: a group hug which does not end until the little ones are laughing and affectionate.

6. Pray with them about it, but don't wait until they are mad at their siblings. Every time you pray, including bedtime and meals, ask God to show them creative ways to love others.

7. Read storybooks or make up bedtime stories about children who are kind and compassionate servants.

8. Give them greater affirmation when you see them love and serve than when they hit a homerun. When they love and serve, allow them to hear you brag to others about it.

9. Do not permit ANY unkind words in your family, ie: no derogatory names, no making fun, no teasing, or belittling of any kind.

10. Model service and kind speech in your marriage. Many have said that the best way for children to learn to love is to be around two parents loving each other.

---

[39] 1 John 4:19

HOW CAN PARENTS RESTORE LOST LOVE AND AFFECTION IN A FAMILY? (Particularly with adolescent aged children)

1. Make it a top goal to express love to your children.[40]

   • Be affectionate toward them, whether it is natural for you or not.

   • Discipline yourself to smile at them. None of us responds well to someone who communicates continual mistrust and suspicion. May your countenance become inviting!

   • Affirm them when they do well. Express to them that you knew they would succeed. Listen to yourself: do you correct them more than you affirm them?

2. Accept them for who they are.

   • They are who they are. You may not like their values, but those values reflect who they actually are. Your constant vocal disapproval will likely not change them – only make them hide their true feelings.

   • Listen to yourself – do you communicate to them that you are never completely pleased, satisfied, or content with them or their efforts? Is it possible your careful scrutinizing has left them feeling that they can never measure up, like they can never succeed? Have you led them to believe they are a big disappointment to you?

---

[40] *Rom 2:4 Or do you show contempt for the riches of his kindness, tolerance and patience, not realizing that God's kindness leads you toward repentance?* (Also 1 John 4:19)

• Consider that your adolescent may be resistant to your leadership, only because they felt so rejected by you that they gave up trying to please you.

• Many middle-aged adults still crave their parents' approval. Do you want your children to be your age and still be waiting for you to say, "I'm proud of you"?

• Consider that many kids, who fail to find their parents' acceptance, will welcome it from the first group or individual who offers it.

• Remember that we are drawn to those who like us, but have little time for those who continually criticize us.

• Many parents who have affectionate relationships with their children assume their children feel accepted. Do not substitute affection for acceptance.

3. If you carry unrelenting resentment toward them, forgive them.

• If you put an exclamation mark at the end of their name, it is time to remove it. None of us are drawn to someone who is always angry with us. You must stop!

• Don't bring up old offenses and repeatedly scold them for them.

Do not call to mind the former things, Or ponder things of the past   Isa 43:18

If you, O LORD, kept a record of sins, O Lord, who could stand? Ps 130:3

> *Then he adds: "Their sins and lawless acts I will remember no more." Heb 10:17*

> *[Love] ... keeps no record of wrongs. 1 Cor 13:5*

• Give them continued fresh starts. Don't think the worst of them, continually guessing their motives to be evil. Love hopes the best.[41] Give them the benefit of the doubt.

> *Be kind and compassionate to one another, forgiving each other, just as in Christ God forgave you. Eph 4:32*

> *Therefore judge nothing before the appointed time; wait till the Lord comes. He will bring to light what is hidden in darkness and will expose the motives of men's hearts. At that time each will receive his praise from God. 1 Cor 4:5*

• Remember that abiding bitterness will destroy you and them.

> *... that no bitter root grows up to cause trouble and defile many. Heb 12:15*

> *"In your anger do not sin" : Do not let the sun go down while you are still angry, 27 and do not give the devil a foothold. Eph 4:26-27*

• Ask forgiveness of them for your resentment.

> *"Therefore, if you are offering your gift at the altar and there remember that your brother has something against you, 24 leave your gift there in front of the altar. First go and be reconciled to your brother; then come and offer your gift. Mat 5:23-24*

• Do not justify your anger. Coercion with rage is a fleshly effort to achieve a spiritual end. We imagine

---

[41] 1 Cor 13:7

that they will see our anger and say to themselves, "Oh, my, what have I done to drive my otherwise sane mother so crazy. I should stop and examine myself." Yet, most people, when they are being verbally assaulted, do not think selfless thoughts. They are too distracted with thoughts of survival and self-preservation.

for the wrath of man does not produce the righteousness of God. James 1:20

4. Listen to them.

• As they approach adolescence begin to give them opportunities to share their heart with you.

• Listen to their feelings without immediately giving them the correction you think they need.

• Be trustworthy with their heart. None of us is willing to risk sharing vulnerable feelings with someone who will attack us with what we share.

• Share with them weaknesses or struggles you are having in your own life.

Parents, just as God does not intend that the Christian life be burdensome,[42] neither should our parenting. If we are weighed down just trying to survive our children, or if we daily struggle just to tolerate them, we are falling short of God's calling for us. We will always be miserable and our children will not easily

---

[42] *Mat 11:29 Take my yoke upon you and learn from me, for I am gentle and humble in heart, and you will find rest for your souls. 30 For my yoke is easy and my burden is light."*

be trained. God does not want us just to endure our kids or merely put up with them – He wants us to aggressively love them! There is a vast difference. When we properly love our children God is glorified and our families reap great blessings. Remember, as Jesus told his followers – when we obey his commandment to love, our joy will be full.[43]

---

[43] *John 15:10 If you obey my commands, you will remain in my love, just as I have obeyed my Father's commands and remain in his love. 11 I have told you this so that my joy may be in you and that your joy may be complete. 12 My command is this: Love each other as I have loved you.*

16

Getting a Fresh Start

"Because of the Lord's great love we are not consumed, for his compassions never fail. 23 They are new every morning ..." Lamentation 3:22-23

Sometimes when parents reach the conclusion of this book they are aggravated at themselves or their children. They feel convicted that they have been slack in their parenting and are convinced that their children have gotten away with too much. Has that happened to you? Are you now determined to change things at home? Are you feeling intense and ready for action? Good, but be careful! Before you attempt to change your parenting, first consider the following thoughts:

- *Plan a strategy with your spouse.*
  Before you go into action, discuss your plans with your mate. If possible, both parents should read this book before one begins implementing anything new. If the children sense there is disharmony between parents, they will play them one against the other.

- *Call a meeting.*
  In order to begin implementing proper training, it is important that parents call a meeting with their children to explain the changes that will be occurring in the way the home is run. Make sure they

understand the new standards and the consequences for violations. That way they do not become resentful for suddenly being held to new standards without forewarning. They know exactly what is happening, why it is happening, and the kinds of changes they should expect.

- *Ask their forgiveness.*
  It will be important to begin your meeting by apologizing for failing with your parenting in the past. You have not properly prepared them for maturity, and asking their forgiveness is in order. This will give you a fresh start and establish the basis for the forthcoming changes.

- *Warn them of possible inconsistencies.*
  Be sure to tell them that as you are relearning your job, you may have blind spots, and therefore may not notice every time they violate a new rule. Warn them that they are not to interpret your lack of action to mean that the new standard is now off.

- *Go slow and watch your anger!*
  I want to restate what I said in the preface. Keep in mind that our children are a product of our training, whether by intent or neglect. They are only the way they are, because we have not yet finished their training. If the children are not learning fast enough, and the training does not seem to be working, then it is time to look for blind spots in our approach, and not time for greater harshness. Children respond best to alert, loving, consistent discipline – not to angry, "don't mess with me, kid" parenting.

- *Remember, "untraining" is not easy.*
  The repentant parent must remember that the enforcement of new rules can be difficult, because half of the training will be *undoing* the negative training you have done thus far.

- *Plan for the possibility of several intense days of frequent chastisement.*
  Some children submit easily, but others enjoy being in charge and may not so willingly release control of the home. They must learn right away, however, that you mean business. You may even consider limiting outside commitments for several days or taking a few days off from work, so you can devote yourself fully to consistent discipline.

To summarize a few ideas from chapter 15 – keep in mind that most of us find it easier to follow the leadership of one who likes us. Your children must *know* of your affection for them. Affirm your children for their successes, do not always think the worst of them, and speak hopefully to them. Watch your countenance. Do your children see you scowling suspiciously at them every time they walk into the room? Scowling communicates to them mistrust – that you assume the worst of them. It is highly unmotivating to please someone who thinks the worst of you. Discipline yourself to greet your kids with a smile. You *do* love your children, so let it leak out through your teeth. You may be amazed how differently they respond to you.

Publications and tape sets by Reb Bradley

Biblical Insights into Child Training: Establishing control in the home and raising godly children – *8 tape set with syllabus*

Preparing Your Children for COURTSHIP and MARRIAGE: *From toddlers to teens* – *6 tape set with syllabus*

Effective Parenting of Teens: What the Bible says about raising teenagers – *6 tape set with syllabus*

Bringing Your Children to an Early Maturity: Reversing the influence of modern culture and youth groups on adolescents *2 tape set with syllabus*

SAVING THE NEXT GENERATION: *Equipping Your Children as Warriors for Christ* – *2 tape set with syllabus*

The Delightful Family – Help in strengthening family bonds and making your home a place of joy – *2 tape set with syllabus*

When Family Becomes an Idol – Helping parents from going too far in elevating their families – *1 tape with outline*

Brother Sister Relationships – Teaching our sons and daughters to honor each other as men and women – *2 tape set with syllabus*

Happiness in Marriage: Discovering the blessing God intended – *8 tape set with syllabus*

The Biblical Path to Mental and Emotional Health Powerful series revealing Jesus' path to wholeness – *12 tape set with syllabus*

For these materials or others, contact your source for this book, or request a complete catalog from Family Ministries:

FAMILY MINISTRIES   PO Box 266   Sheridan, CA 95681
(530) 633-9923   Credit card order line 800-545-1729
www.familyministries.com